THE DIVESTITURE OPTION

Recent Titles from Quorum Books

THE DIVESTITURE OPTION

A Guide for Financial and Corporate Planning Executives

RICHARD J. SCHMIDT

Q

QUORUM BOOKS

New York · Westport, Connecticut · London

Library of Congress Cataloging-in-Publication Data

Schmidt, Richard J. (Richard John)
  The divestiture option.

  Includes bibliographical references.
  1. Corporate divestiture. I. Title.
HD2746.6.S36 1990   658.1'6   89–10879
ISBN 0–89930–397–8 (lib. bdg.)

British Library Cataloguing in Publication Data is available.

Library of Congress Catalog Card Number: 89–10879
ISBN: 0–89930–397–8

First published in 1990 by Quorum Books

Greenwood Press, Inc.
88 Post Road West, Westport, Connecticut 06881

Printed in the United States of America

The paper used in this book complies with the
Permanent Paper Standard issued by the National
Information Standards Organization (Z39.48–1984).

10 9 8 7 6 5 4 3 2 1

Contents

Acknowledgments

I wish to thank Guy Banville for his early support of this project, and Tom Gannon who saw it through to completion. Special thanks are due to the best in-house editor and proofreader
a writer could have, my wife, Shauna.

THE DIVESTITURE OPTION

1

Major Acquisition and Divestiture Activity

During the 1950s and 1960s, the acquisition of one business by another to form ever larger corporations was an accepted business practice. Dynamic, fast-growth companies were combining with slow-growth, mature corporations for a counterbalancing effect during business cycle swings. However, with the complex interactions of the U.S. and foreign economies, it was very difficult to identify exactly countercyclical businesses. Even when the countercyclical businesses were identified, it was difficult for diversifying corporations to construct a balanced corporate combination where the variable returns of individual businesses were balanced.

Business combinations have been more frequent with varying popularity in recent economic periods. Corporations have reacted differently during these periods, which include (1) the 1970s recession effects; (2) the diversification analysis period; (3) the divestiture period; and (4) transaction sophistication.

The economics of scale and the "bigger is better" concept had driven managements to form more complex heterogeneous business combinations, believing that management skills were truly transferable regardless of the specific business or industry involved. If management could operate a service operation, then, corporate management thought, the same managers could just as effectively manage a manufacturing or distribution organization. If they could manage a minerals production corporation in the West, they could manage a garment manufacturer in New York City.

Economic retrenchments and downturns showed that the management abilities necessary to successfully direct a "smokestack" industry manufacturing company through reduced business activity were not the same skills necessary to manage the survival, for example, of a complex financial services corporation or a soft goods manufacturer.

THE 1970s RECESSION EFFECTS

The conglomerate era continued to build until the recession of 1974–75. Corporations practiced a near-slavish emphasis on high market shares as the key to corporate success. Management expected the increased share to result in an increased return on investment. Kathryn Harrigan of Columbia University said, "There was a lot of silliness as corporations spent wildly to be the No.1 or the No. 2 in an industry. There's been a huge asset buildup because they spend unwisely. We're going through another upchuck period (1980s) of all that junk." And Lyman Hamilton, former head of ITT and president of Tramco Enterprises, said, "Diversified corporations haven't, on balance, proved that they can outperform their single-product competitors."[1]

Inflationary pressures in the late 1960s pushed fixed asset valuation higher than previously experienced. This provided higher valued bases for secured financing that supplied the backing for mergers. Mergers and acquisitions had peaked in 1969 when the relatively mild recession of 1969–70 forced some corporations to reasses their diversification philosophies. The drop in the stock market in 1970 precipitated the decrease in the number of corporate mergers. The net number of announced mergers and acquisitions has significantly declined from the peak year of 1969 as shown in Table 1.1.

In the 1970s corporations began to divest some of their prior merger partners because of many factors. Higher interest rates on borrowed funds required more effective asset usage, and management found it could not manage widely different businesses. Capital-intensive industries required far different man-

Table 1.1

Years	Net Number of Merger and Acquisition Announcements
1967	2,975
1968	4,462
1969	6,107
1970	5,152
1971	4,608
1972	4,801
1973	4,040

Source: *Mergerstat Review* (Chicago: W. T. Grimm & Co., 1987), p. 103.

agement know-how than labor-intensive operations. Companies were forced to sell selected assets to raise capital during recessionary periods. The concept of a conglomerate being able to counterbalance cyclic economic swings proved to be no defense during recessionary drops in the economy.

Accounting techniques added to the acquisition period by developing the pooling of interest method of accounting for merged corporations. Acquisitors could combine the sales and earnings of the combined firms, thereby increasing the earnings per share of the acquisitor. The increase in large-scale consolidations was a management response to a rapidly changing environment. With high inflation and cost of capital, mergers became the management method to maintain high growth rates.

DIVERSIFICATION ANALYSIS PERIOD

The discovery that broad and sometimes random diversification would not protect a corporation during a recession brought home the point that a corporation required at least a minimum concept of what business the corporation was operating. Successful acquisitions, according to one report, "Resulted because the acquirer was able to leverage skills and assets to offset the acquisition premium through operational expertise, general management skills, and financial engineering. On the other hand, companies that relied exclusively on financial engineering, typically changing financial structure to finance an acquisition, were unsuccessful in almost every case."[2] The conglomerate movement focused on short-term earnings objectives rather than long-term financial and diversification goals. Anticipated earnings increases became illusory and management found it difficult to understand, much less manage all the new businesses.

In December 1976, under prodding from the Securities and Exchange Commission, the Financial Accounting Standards Board, the financial accounting reporting standard setting body, issued Statement on Financial Accounting Standards No. 14, *Financial Reporting for Segments of a Business Enterprise*. This statement required publicly held corporations to report assets held and income generated by disaggregated corporate segments of similar products and services. For the first time, public disclosure was made of many business segments that were obviously unprofitable. The disclosure forced management into explaining to stockholders why certain portions of the corporation were producing low returns on the stockholders' invested capital.

DIVESTITURE PERIOD

When this new financial reporting requirement was combined with the recession that began in 1970–71 and reappeared in 1974–75, diversified corporations created by earlier acquisitions joined the divestiture list. Divestitures became one means to raise badly needed capital and reduce operating concerns. Table 1.2 shows the increase in the number of corporate divestitures during this period.

Management became aware of the fact that redirection was necessary if individual corporations were to continue as healthy business entities into the 1980s and 1990s. Acquisitions continued as a business strategy but were joined by planned divestitures. As Table 1.3 shows, both corporate acquisitions and divestitures have been significant.

Stock and debt made mergers more complex than strictly cash

Table 1.2

Years	Number of Corporate Divestitures
1968	557
1969	801
1970	1,401
1971	1,920
1972	1,770
1973	1,557
1974	1,331
1975	1,236

Source: *Mergerstat Review* (Chicago: W. T. Grimm & Co., 1986), p. 68.

transactions and introduced the concept of complex merger exchanges. The number and complexity of mergers have increased to the point where stock and debt are extremely valuable factors in consummating the acquisitions.

Table 1.3

Years	Net Mergers and Acquisition Announcements	Number of Corporate Divestitures
1980	1,889	666
1981	2,395	830
1982	2,346	875
1983	2,533	932
1984	2,543	900
1985	3,001	1,218
1986	3,336	1,259
1987	2,032	807

Source: *Mergerstat Review* (Chicago: W. T. Grimm & Co., 1987), p. 104.

In 1987 merger and acquisition transactions were nearly evenly split between cash, stock, and combination exchanges as:

Cash Only Transactions	41%
Stock Swaps	34%
Combination of Cash, Stock and Debt	24%
Debt Only	1%
	———
All Transactions	100%[3]

Although the largest U.S. corporate divestiture, $2.8 billion for the divestiture of the diversified retailing firm Montgomery Ward from Mobil Corporation to General Electric Co. in 1988, is significantly less than the largest U.S. corporate acquisition, $13.44 billion acquisition of Kraft Inc. by Philip Morris Inc. in 1988, the number and size of the transactions are large enough to make divestitures a major factor in the American and international economies.

TRANSACTION SOPHISTICATION

With both the stock and debt markets as well as increased international economic sophistication and experience, corporate management began to weigh alternatives, including strategic divestiture plans, to eliminate unsuccessful sections of the business, rather than just spinning off an occasional unprofitable segment.

As corporate acquisition development became more advanced, cash was found to be less a problem in reaching corporate success than technical competence, and the latter less critical than managerial ability. Management had demonstrated by its lack of success in many business combination cases that it couldn't be assumed that management ability could rise to any occasion. "The diversification of American industry is marked by hundreds of instances in which a company strong in one endeavor lacked the ability to manage an enterprise requiring different skills. Opportunism without competence is a path to fairyland."[4] Corporate strategy became the summation of a series of product and market decisions.

Creative financing methods became popular. Assignment of both debt and assets to divested segments became a common practice in divestitures. The 1980s became an era of extremely large, $20 billion, takeovers and nearly as large, $2.8 billion, divestitures. Determinants of an important alternative, corporate divestitures, needed refinement and analysis.

During this same period, large foreign corporations acquired major U.S. corporations. British, French, and to a lesser extent Italian companies had become more active in looking to the United States for profitable business expansion. The United States with its continual national deficit spending policies contributed to a declining dollar situation that made many U.S. divestitures financially attractive to foreign investors.

A new, aggressive industry developed. Acquisition and divestiture advising by investment bankers or specialized brokers grew to a multibillion-dollar industry. In 1988, the six largest investment banks advising on merger, acquisition, and divestiture transactions were:[5]

Investment Bank	Transaction Values
Goldman, Sachs & Co.	$92 billion
First Boston	$72.7 billion
Morgan Stanley	$68.1 billion
Shearson	$56.9 billion
Salomon Brothers Inc.	$42 billion
Wasserstein, Perella & Co.	$38.1 billion

Acquisitions and divestitures had moved permanently into the realms of mega-billion dollar business transactions.

ACQUISITION AND DIVESTITURE PERIOD SUMMATION

The period of the 1950s through the 1980s has been one of the frequent forming and dissolving of business corporation combinations. Corporations have reacted to economic recessions by merging or divesting. Rapid moves into business diversification brought many corporations products and services they were ill-prepared to handle. Further divestitures and combinations have followed until the development of complex financial sophistication in the late 1980s has increased the magnitude of both acquisitions and divestitures.

2

Business Environmental Changes

Besides general economic events, corporations have to confront many economic phenomena that can affect their very existence. Specific economic environmental changes affecting the corporate existence include:

1. Corporate life cycle
2. Changes in market demand
3. Appearance of replacement products in the market
4. Increased foreign and domestic competition
5. Obsolete manufacturing facilities
6. Changing corporate goals and objectives
7. Government antitrust activity

When a corporate segment is involved in an economic downturn, corporation officers often look to both sales expansion and cost containment or reduction. A fluctuation in a business' economic segment can be caused by a number of factors, including international trade activities; the introduction of a new competitive product; government economic intervention or inactivity; general inflationary or deflationary trends; changes in domestic competition; changes in management's business goals; or changes in consumer tastes. An economic downturn may catch the management unaware because optimism generally is the basic assumption for planning corporation projections. An economic downturn can initiate internal reviews and corporate self-evaluations that result in significant changes in the way the corporation does its business.

CORPORATE LIFE CYCLE

Nearly every elementary economic text contains the product life cycle concept. The concept traces a product from conception, through birth, growth, maturity, decline, and its eventual death. All of these stages are shown as a function of time. Many products have experienced a rapid decline from maturity to total demise. A corporation, as the aggregate of many products and services, may follow such a curve. The principal difference between the product and corporation curves is the amount of time between the initiation of a product's conception and death, and the organization's incorporation and possible corporate discontinuance. Whereas a product may last 5 or 20 years, an ongoing corporation often exists from 10 to 60 years or more. An example of a corporate life cycle relationship is shown in Figure 2.1.

The dynamics of the life cycle can change a corporation's attitude toward any particular business activity. When the market is expanding, management is confident of its ability to successfully meet the new challenges. However, when the market stabilizes or declines, management may lose confidence in its ability to make the decisions necessary to operate in the changing market. Many factors can influence the business environment, not all of them favorably.

MARKET CHANGES

Changes in the market for a corporation's product have far-ranging impacts on the corporation. When the corporation's product markets are growing, management is confident they can succeed. Market changes indicate that management should take some corrective action. Increases in demand require production increases, product allocation, distribution system reviews, inventory adjustments, and/or price adjustments. Mar-

Figure 2.1
A Corporate Life Cycle Relationship

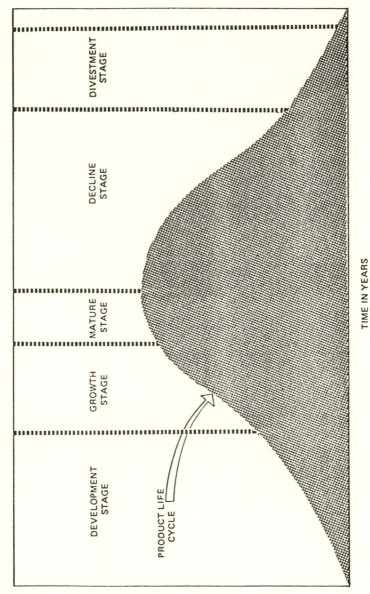

DEVELOPMENT STAGE

GROWTH STAGE

MATURE STAGE

DECLINE STAGE

DIVESTMENT STAGE

PRODUCT LIFE CYCLE

Measure of Performance

TIME IN YEARS

ket decreases may threaten the very existence of management if the declining trends cannot be reduced or stabilized, even at a lower level than previously acceptable. However, some market changes are beyond the control of management. For example, the federal government has reduced the amount of payments made for home health care. In response, Avon Products Inc. agreed to sell its struggling Foster Home Health Care division because of its decreased market. Foster was the nation's largest supplier of home care equipment for respiratory therapy. Avon had purchased it only four years before agreeing to sell it. Proceeds of the sale were reallocated to other corporate divisions whose markets have not been affected by decreased government payment programs.[1]

REPLACEMENT PRODUCTS

The introduction of a competitive product into the marketplace can displace a product from a previously thought secure market niche. Examples such as plastics for steel in automobiles, microcircuits for vacuum tubes in electronics, and natural and bottled gas and electricity for coal in residential and commercial heating demonstrate the susceptibility of products to market replacement. Organizations react to such changes in many ways, including modifying old products, developing new ones, repricing, and corporate redirection away from the affected marketplace. Corporate redirection can consist of diversifying to quickly acquire new products. Divestitures of unwanted segments may be necessary before the acquisition in order to finance it, or after the merger to sell unwanted segments of the acquired company.

FOREIGN AND DOMESTIC COMPETITION

International trade has increased the number and ability of competing producers. Domestic corporations have been forced to become more competitive because of this foreign competition. Existing corporations, confident in their corporate style, went to work one morning to find a new or strengthened competitor serving former customers. America has responded by improving its communication systems, government sponsorship of defense research and production, and imaginative financing of new ventures. These have added to the ability of U.S. companies to compete in the international marketplace.

Trade barriers have been tried over the years, but they have not had a lasting, favorable impact on domestic producers. Recent federal administrations have moved away from trade restrictions and toward free-trade approaches in solving trade disputes. Therefore, market changes and the affects on individual corporations must be solved by the individual companies affected, not by government actions.

OBSOLETE FACILITIES

With manufacturing asset intensive industries, technical and physical obsolescence becomes a critical factor in maintaining cost and quality competitiveness. The U.S. steel and automobile industries are well-known examples of entire industries whose manufacturing facilities became nearly obsolete because they were not replaced with newly developed technology. In these two industries, foreign competition entered the market with higher quality and lower cost products than could be produced in the antiquated U.S. facilities.

Besides equipment obsolescence, employee productivity concepts can become obsolete when compared with competitive producers. The introduction of employee unions, the rigidity of work rules, or wage scales may drastically change the economics of a segment's operation. The migration of the skilled work force away from the facility area may create unfilled positions that seriously decrease efficiency. In some U.S. areas, these factors have caused corporations to consider divestiture as well as other alternatives including plant shutdown and operational moves.

CHANGING CORPORATION GOALS AND OBJECTIVES

Because a corporation is a group of assets including its officers and employees, the goals and objectives of its people often change with time. Changes in the economy and markets also may initiate changes in corporate goals. As persons in the corporation age, quit, and retire, new employees bring with them new ideas on the direction the corporation should move. The new goals may require a different mix of assets than the corporation presently has maintained. Therefore, purchases and sales of corporate assets become necessary to work toward the changed goals.

In 1989 Gulf & Western Inc. planned to auction its large finance subsidiary, the Associates, for between $3 and $5 billion. Management plans to build an even-bigger entertainment and communications powerhouse. Although the Associates was highly profitable, it did not fit the rapidly consolidating global communications business. The prospect of a sudden infusion of proceeds from the Associates sale will probably be spent in acquiring independent entertainment concerns that might complement the Paramount and Simon & Schuster components of Gulf & Western. To reflect the new direction, the company has been renamed Paramount Communications Corporation.[2]

When a corporation becomes financially troubled, the survival instinct of its management may supersede other corporate goals. In the 1970s LTV Corporation and Boise Cascade changed from a pursuit of growth and expansion in diversified markets to one of simple survival in one principal industry. After World War II, steel companies sought control of ore and coal sources. However, attitudes toward the importance of company control of raw materials changed significantly. Altered goals, often built on survival instincts and the influence of a corporate life cycle, have influenced the way a corporation has viewed environmental changes.[3]

GOVERNMENT ANTITRUST ACTIVITY

Antitrust actions can adversely affect all aspects of the corporation. Planning to avoid the adverse government intervention is very difficult. Government legislative, judicial, and executive interpretations of commercial antitrust activity changes over time. Changes in decision-making personnel and the economic environment alters the definition of what anticompetitive business activity is. Antitrust has changed. It is no longer an angry and frightened populist movement fighting the growing power of big business. Today it is a bureaucratically enforced set of legal rules. Modern antitrust law shapes the kinds of mergers a firm may undertake, but its aim is to prevent monopoly power, not the growth of corporations. Recent federal policy is based on the opposition to only the anticompetitive aspects of mergers. The antitrust laws can also stop a divestiture-acquisition combination. In 1988 Schering-Plough Corporation was interested in paying $195 million for several vision care businesses from Cooper Companies. After reviewing the proposed purchase, the Federal Trade Commission planned to ask a federal court to stop it based on antitrust considerations. Schering-Plough withdrew from the transaction because of regulatory concerns. The cash-poor Cooper management, which needed the funds to pay down its debt load, continued to look for a divestiture buyer for its optometric business.[4]

A corporation need not develop its own antitrust standards; the state and federal governments have established the standards, and they communicate the essential information through their channels and apply them to a particular corporate activity. In foreign situations, governments may expropriate and nationalize business assets to make their point.

In the recent case of AT&T, Federal Judge Greene wrote in his opinion on why he would not dismiss the antitrust suit against AT&T, "The motion to dismiss is denied. The testimony and the documentary evidence adduced by the government demonstrate that the Bell System has violated the antitrust laws in a number of ways over a lengthy period of time. On the three principal factual issues . . . the evidence sustains the government's basic contentions, and the burden is on defendants to refute the actual showings made in the government's case." When AT&T contended that antitrust standards were in conflict with its historic regulatory position, Judge Greene answered, "By the mid-1970's the FCC had clearly begun to promote competition in telecommunications . . . AT&T had an obligation to follow the more recent FCC policy rather than the Commission's previous policies which may have suited it better."[5] Public policy on commercial competitiveness was determined by a federal agency interpretation of the business environment while monopoly antitrust laws remained intact.

ENVIRONMENTAL SUMMARY

Changes in the business environment may cause management to review their corporate position in the marketplace. The corporation has a definite life cycle beginning at conception and ending at its demise, but the particular length of life is determined by market factors and the corporation's willingness and ability to change to meet the newly modified markets.

Environmental factors including replacement products, competition, obsolete facilities, changing corporate goals, and governmental antitrust action can cause corporations to react with mergers, retrenchment, and divestitures.

3

Antitrust Laws

Antitrust activity has been a significant factor in creating business situations from which corporate divestiture has resulted. Business antitrust laws have endured both intense interest and periods of near complete neglect. From an early history of government intervention into unfavorable business practices, antitrust laws evolved in England and were slowly adopted in the United States. Four significant antitrust laws were passed to counter a growing trend of socially undesirable business concentrations. The development is traced from:

1. Early history
2. Early antitrust common law in England
3. The need for antitrust activity in the United States
4. The Sherman Act
5. The Clayton Act
6. The Robinson-Patman Act
7. Post-World War II monopoly fears
8. The Celler-Kefauver Act

EARLY HISTORY

Government activity toward the business practices commonly associated with antisocial activities such as price fixing, monopolies, and the allocation of markets has been traced to A.D. 483. The Roman Emperor Zeno wrote an edict to the Praetorian Prefect of Constantinople directing:

that no one may presume to exercise a monopoly of any kind of clothing, or of fish, or of any other thing serving for food, or for any other use, whatever its nature may be, either of his own authority or under a rescript of an emperor already procured, or that may hereafter be procured, or under an Imperial decree, or under a rescript signed by our Majesty; nor may any persons combine or agree in unlawful meetings, that different kinds of merchandise may not be sold at a less price than they may have agreed upon among themselves.[1]

EARLY ANTITRUST COMMON LAW IN ENGLAND

The federal U.S. antitrust laws trace their origin to the common law of England. In 1599, Sir Edward Coke, a prominent English courtroom lawyer, speaker of Parliament, and Queen Elizabeth's attorney general, argued the first recorded antitrust case, *Davenant v. Hurdis*. The case was based on a law that required every tailor's guild member who sent cloth to be finished by outside labor to have at least one-half of the work done by a tailor guild member. The defendant, who was a member of the tailor's guild, refused to pay the guild when he sent cloth out to be sewn. He was subsequently fined and his goods seized to pay the fine. Coke argued that the law was illegal, and such a law might create monopoly powers against the public good. The court agreed, holding that "a rule of such nature as to bring all trade or traffic into the hands of one company, or one person, and to exclude all others, is illegal."[2]

In 1603 the English case of *Darcy v. Allein* took the monopoly concept one step further by establishing the principle that even a royal grant by patent was invalid if it created a monopoly.[3] The Statute of Monopolies of 1624 declared all monopolies and grants illegal except those created by cities, towns, corporations, trading companies, and guilds. The 1624 statute slowed the movement toward freer enterprise, but a 1711 case, *Mitchell v. Reynolds*, weakened opportunities to create sanctioned monopolies. Lord Macclesfield wrote the court's opinion, which became known as the Macclesfield Rule. It stated that a contract in restraint of trade would be valid only if the restraint was "particular" and the contract "appears to be made upon a good and adequate consideration, so as to make it a proper and useful contract."[4]

Later English court decisions added to the confusion on whether and under what conditions enterprise monopolies would be permitted under common law. By 1890 English common law was an ineffective limitation on monopolies and restraints of trade. In the United States, state courts looked to the earlier English court decisions as they began to formulate their own rules to curtail destructive monopolies and restraints of trade.

THE NEED FOR ANTITRUST ACTIVITY IN THE UNITED STATES

During the same period, a uniquely American institution was developed, the business trust, which was an informal group of companies closely collaborating to benefit their own positions at the expense of the public good. The Standard Oil Company Trust, the American Cotton Oil Trust, the Sugar Trust, the National Linseed Oil Trust, the Whiskey Trust, and the National Lead Trust were the more prominent. Their ruthless methods of competition enraged the public and dragged business morality to the lowest point in U.S. history. For example, the National Cash Register Company was formed during this period and was described by Clair Wilcox as:

The National Cash Register Co., organized in 1882, set out deliberately to destroy its competitors. It hired employees away from them. It bribed their employees and the employees of common carriers and telephone and telegraph companies to spy on them and disclose their business secrets. It spread false rumors concerning their solvency. It instructed its agents to misrepresent the quality of their goods, interfere with their sales, and damage the mechanism of their machines in establishments where they were in use. It publicly displayed their cash registers under labels which read, "Junk." It made, and sold at cost, inferior machines called "Knockers," which it represented to be just as good as theirs. It threatened to bring suit against them and their customers for alleged infringement of patent rights. It induced their customers to cancel their orders by publishing lists of defunct competitors and by exhibiting in a "graveyard" at its factory samples of machines which they had formerly made.[5]

THE SHERMAN ACT

In 1888 Senator Sherman introduced a bill designed to eliminate the abuses of trusts by providing antitrust restrictions introduced years earlier in the common law. After much bitter debate and compromise, the 1889 reintroduction of the antitrust bill was signed by President Harrison on July 1, 1890. The Sherman Act was immediately labelled as both the law to end the trusts and an ineffective, weak, and badly worded mock law that would accomplish nothing.

Problems of implementation began immediately. Lack of staff and funds in the attorney general's office coupled with the lack of presidential interest in enforcing the law were present through the administrations of Harrison, Cleveland, and McKinley. The few cases tried under the Sherman Act pointed out the broad language of the act, the lack of definitive judicial interpretations, and the presence of legal loopholes within the law itself. Trusts were not destroyed by the Sherman Act. In fact, Senator William Thompson of Kansas was quoted as saying that between 1898 and 1908 there were 628 new trusts formed from 9,877 independent companies. He stated this was the greatest amount of trust formation in our history.[6]

In turn, the trusts began to use the act to crush labor strikes and union organizational activity. Between 1890 to 1914, 101 cases were filed where federal courts issued injunctions against labor organizations, although the Sherman Act was not intended to apply to labor combinations.[7]

In 1911 the U.S. Supreme Court decided that the Standard Oil Company of New Jersey was violative of the Sherman Act and ordered its dismemberment. The Court concluded that not all combinations in restraint of trade are illegal. Only those that are "unreasonable" were violative of the act. The Court took upon itself the determination as to whether a restraint was reasonable or unreasonable. This was the first significant application of antitrust activity that resulted in the forced divestiture of business segments.

THE CLAYTON ACT

Congress reacted by passing the Clayton Act in 1914 to strengthen the Sherman Act. The Clayton Act prohibits specific trade practices and condemns practices whose effect *may be* substantially to lessen competition. This is a strengthening of the Sherman language, which prohibits those restraints that *in fact* unreasonably restrain trade.[8]

One month prior to the passage of the Clayton Act, the Federal Trade Commission Act was passed to supplement the Sherman Act. The FTC Act provided a commission with the ability and power to establish reliable guidelines for antitrust activity.

When a new wave of mergers emerged in the mid-1920s, the transactions created large competitors such as Bethlehem Steel, which challenged the existing dominance of monopoly firms like U.S. Steel. Large size became a social and economic ally against the monopolies. Antitrust legislation posed no threat to the new giants.

THE ROBINSON-PATMAN ACT

The fourth congressional act of importance to antitrust and divestiture was the 1936 Robinson-Patman Act. This statute amends the Clayton Act by providing civil remedies through government enforcement and private triple damage actions. It bars discriminatory pricing where specified competitive injury may result; prohibits a seller from paying brokerage or commission or giving any discount in lieu of brokerage to a buyer; and prohibits a seller from making any payment to a customer as compensation for services provided by the buyer in connection with goods purchased unless such payment is available on proportionably equal terms to all other competing customers. Big business had become commonplace in the United States and thus less frightening to the public mind. Nevertheless, the three acts constitute the principle legislative foundation to control unacceptable, competition-reducing business practices.

POST—WORLD WAR II MONOPOLY FEARS

World War II reawakened the fear of big business. Americans believed that Nazi Germany and Imperial Japan would not have been able to wage the world war without the strong industrial base created by the leaders of the huge, concentrated industries who supported the militaristic policies of their governments. If Germany and Japan had been more pluralistic and democratic, their populations would have been able to resist the tyranny that led to war. In this atmosphere, Congress passed an aggressive antimerger law in 1950, the Celler-Kefauver Act.

Emanuel Celler, a member of the House of Representatives, stated for the Congressional Record:

I want to point out the danger of this trend toward more and better combines. I read from a report filed with the Secretary of War as to the history of cartelization and concentration of industry in Germany: "Germany under the Nazi set-up built up a great series of industrial monopolies in steel, rubber, coal and other materials. The monopolies soon got control of Germany, brought Hitler to power and forced virtually the whole world into war.[9]

Senator Estes Kefauver gave an insight behind the Celler-Kefauver Act in terms reminiscent of Senator Sherman in the 1880s when Kefauver added to the Congressional Record the following:

Through monopolistic mergers the people are losing the power to direct their own economic welfare. When they lose that power they also lose the means to direct their political future. I am not an alarmist, but the history of what has taken place in other nations where mergers and concentrations have placed economic control in the hands of a very few people is too clear to pass over easily. A point is reached, and we are rapidly reaching that point in this country, where the public steps in to take over when concentration and monopoly gain too much power. The taking over by the public through its government always follows one or two methods and has one or two political results. It either results in a Fascist state or the nationalization of industries and thereafter a Socialist or Communist state.[10]

THE CELLER-KEFAUVER ACT

The 1950 Celler-Kefauver Act was an amendment of Section 7 of the Clayton Act. Asset purchase mergers that reduced competition "in any line of commerce" and that "may substantially lessen competition" were prohibited. For the first time, the antimerger law applied to the acquisition of noncompeting firms if the merger is likely to reduce competition.

The Celler-Kefauver Act eliminated almost all large-scale mergers between competing firms and between giant firms and their suppliers or customers. Assets acquired in these mergers declined from one-half of all mergers in 1950 to 20 percent by 1965.[11] However, the act had little effect on unrelated firm acquisitions. Interpretation required some showing of competitive harm before it was applied to a proposed merger. As with the Clayton Act, the Celler-Kefauver Act proved effective in stopping the type of mergers seen in prior years, but not the mergers of the late 1960s.

In a 1960 article, law professor Derek Bok argued that the combination of economic learning and the legalities of the Celler-Kefauver Act would lead to the adoption of a series of rules based on the number of competitors selling a product. The court would assume that if few competitors sold a product, a merger between large firms would reduce competition. The courts adopted this general approach, which has resulted in antitrust litigation in merger cases not considering the specific economic impact of the challenged merger. The litigation centers on defining the product, how many firms sell the product, and the percentage of sales belonging to the merging firms.[12] This theory for use in the courts was aided by the lack of organized opposition to the antitrust laws within the economics profession.

In the 1963 case of the *United States v. Philadelphia Bank*, the Supreme Court defined a simplified test of illegal merger activity:

A merger which produces a firm controlling an undue percentage share of the relevant market, and results in a significant increase in the concentration of firms in that market is so inherently likely to lessen competition substantially that it must be enjoined in the absence of evidence clearly showing that the merger is not likely to have such anticompetitive effects.[13]

In a 1966 case the Supreme Court found Von's Grocery Company guilty of violating the Clayton Act's Section 7 because of a growing trend toward market concentration. The proposed merger between the third and sixth largest retail grocery chains in the Los Angeles metropolitan area would have made it the second largest chain with $175,000,000 in annual sales. The merged chain would have controlled 7.5 percent of the market. Citing these facts and noting that the number of single-store grocery stores had declined significantly as well as seeing the number of grocery chains growing from 96 to 150, the Supreme Court held that "these facts alone" were sufficient to demonstrate a violation of Section 7.[14]

Conglomerate acquisitions do not have any direct or immediate effect on market concentrations. The economic and legal questions presented are generally more complex and elusive than those presented by horizontal or vertical mergers. The Supreme Court has used the threats to competition by raising entry barriers, eliminating potential competition, or creating reciprocity opportunities to condemn the antitrust conglomerate activity it has seen. Lower courts, however, have resisted this trend and have often rejected government claims that conglomerate mergers by large corporations violate Section 7 by contributing to the "rising tide of economic concentration in American industry."[15]

ANTITRUST LAW SUMMATION

The early antitrust activity in England soon resulted in English antitrust laws. The United States slowly realized that socially undesirable business activity, particularly monopolies, required antitrust legislation. Worldwide business activities during and after World War II identified the need for even stronger laws to control certain anticompetitive business activity. The four federal acts—Sherman, Clayton, Robinson-Patman, and Celler-Kefauver—provide the basis for antitrust legal action dealing with controlling undesirable corporate mergers.

4

Divestiture and the Implementation of Antitrust Laws

Implementation of the antitrust laws often has resulted in divestiture orders from the courts. The activity is traced as:

1. Antitrust enforcement
2. Corporate structural changes as an antitrust remedy
3. Divestiture not designed as a penalty
4. Legal applications of divestiture in antitrust
5. Williamson economic model
6. Divestiture examples from antitrust applications
7. Postmerger divestiture studies
8. Department of Justice merger guidelines

ANTITRUST ENFORCEMENT

At the federal level, the primary responsibility for the antitrust enforcement is with the Antitrust Division of the Department of Justice. Initiating an antitrust action can begin with information from the Federal Trade Commission, the Securities Exchange Commission, the Federal Bureau of Investigation, Congress, convicted antitrust violators, or a federal grand jury.

Regardless of the source of the information that initiates an antitrust action in either a hearing before one of the applicable commissions or a trial in a federal court, corporate divestiture may be ordered to correct the perceived wrong. Economic theory provides two traditional objections to the perfectly competitive model as a guide to public policy. The first is the theory of "workable competition" proposed by J. M. Clark.[1]

Clark's theory held that socially desirable industrial economic performance will not be obtained by imposing all of the structural conditions of perfect competition. If a particular industry is characterized by the economics of scale, the perfect competitive economic model of many independent firms would lower its economic efficiency. Imposing any one of the conditions of perfect competition on an industry where all of the conditions of perfect competition could not simultaneously be met could harm the industry's economic performance. If the economics of scale dictate few firms in a particular industry, open price quoting could reduce competitive price cutting, which would reduce economic efficiency. When Clark introduced his theory of workable competition, it generated numerous comments and discussions among economists, although it appears trivial by today's international economic standards.

The second objection to the perfectly competitive economic model was the theory of "second best" by J. E. Meade.[2] This theory is founded on the observation that if one of the industries does not produce the optimum results of perfect competition, the attainment of perfect competition in other industries may actually lessen overall economic welfare. If one industry in an economy continues to exercise market power, then efforts by society to attain the results of perfect competition in other sectors of the economy through antitrust policy may be counterproductive and actually lower the value of total output. Although Meade's theory can be mathematically formulated, the decision rules for attaining optimality are so complex and the necessary data so costly to obtain that one investigator labeled it the theory of "counsel of despair."[3]

A combination of both theoretical objections to moving toward perfect competition using antitrust policy has been summarized by the following theorem: "If a strictly laissez-faire policy does not bring about perfect competition in all markets, then it is incorrect economic policy to attempt to achieve perfect competition in the economy as a whole through antitrust enforcement."[4] Therefore, public policy concerning antitrust activity will not strive to reach perfect economic competition. The enforcement of antitrust legislation will be selective to right perceived economic wrongs on a case by case basis.

CORPORATE STRUCTURAL CHANGES AS AN ANTITRUST REMEDY

As an antitrust remedy, the penalty of directed corporate structural change is tied with the economic theory that a market's structure may affect competitive performance. The economic structuralist believes that only through the dissolution of a dominant firm will the competitive conditions of market competition and independent corporate action be assured. If a corporation secures market power by an acquisition, the remedy is to require the divestiture of the acquired firm, thereby restoring the market to its previous and hopefully more competitive condition. This has been referred to as "trust-busting" from the national experience with the early twentieth-century American trusts. Divestiture as a trust-busting device has a record of questionable effectiveness. The railroad baron James Hill was quoted as saying about the value of forced divestiture, "Two certificates of stock are now issued instead of one; they are printed in different colors, and that is the main difference."[5]

DIVESTITURE NOT DESIGNED AS A PENALTY

In United States antitrust law, divestiture is not seen as a penalty for antitrust violations but rather as a remedy to be applied in situations where competition cannot be restored in any other manner. The U.S. Supreme Court has held that in civil antitrust proceedings the courts are not "to punish antitrust violators, and relief must not be punitive."[6] The federal consent decrees with ITT left untouched most of the assets originally listed in the government's complaint with the expressed belief that the directed divestiture of these assets would penalize the stockholders of ITT.[7]

In the 1947 case of the *U.S. v. International Salt Company*, the

Supreme Court emphasized the actual intent behind the use of the antitrust acts: "In an equity suit, the end to be served is not punishment of past transgression, nor is it merely to end specific illegal practices. A public interest served by such civil suits is that they effectively pry open to competition a market that has been closed by defendants' illegal restraints. If this decree accomplishes less than that, the Government has won a lawsuit and lost a cause."[8]

Economic theory expects monopoly power to yield a return on the corporate assets above that expected from a competitive situation. These above-expected returns accrue to the stockholders. The legal guidelines of not penalizing the stockholders in antitrust divestitures therefore are counter to the economic results of who benefits from the prior monopoly position. The monopoly returns may be capitalized in the stock price of the corporation. Anyone purchasing shares of a firm with monopoly power would earn only a normal rate of return. The test of monopoly power would be the loss the capital market registers for the value of the corporation's stock following its carefully directed divestiture. If divestiture took no toll in the corporation's stock price, it is unlikely there was monopoly power.[9]

LEGAL APPLICATIONS OF DIVESTITURE IN ANTITRUST

Divestiture under the antimerger applications of antitrust law has been hampered by the necessity of deciding what the acquiring firm must divest. The legal guideline has been to concentrate on the assets that were acquired in violation of the law. By the time legal divestiture is applied, these assets may be outdated, altered, or integrated into the parent firm. To divest them may be physically impossible or even senseless. For example, after a leading agricultural magazine, *Farm Journal*, acquired its principal rival, *Country Gentlemen*, its gain was the subscription list and the right to solicit unfilled subscriptions. There was essentially nothing to divest after a Clayton Act antitrust violation was found. Separating the offending assets may mean selling them without the human capital to give them any chance for survival as a viable business entity. The problem often has been resolved by selling the assets to another ongoing firm rather than making them a freestanding entity.

THE WILLIAMSON ECONOMIC MODEL

Oliver Williamson devised an economic model comparing the social losses resulting from monopoly and social benefits derived from the economics of scale.[10] Society benefits from an economic standpoint if the gain in the value of resources saved is greater than the loss in consumer's surplus. The Supreme Court touched on one aspect of the Williamson model when they wrote: "Surely one premise of an anti-merger statute . . . is that corporate growth by internal expansion is socially preferable to growth by acquisition."[11] It can be summarized as: most cost-saving advantages of combination are as likely to be available to the acquiring firm through internal expansion as through merger. Internal expansion is not likely to have as adverse an effect upon competition as a business combination. Therefore, an antitrust policy against anticompetitive mergers is not likely to deprive society of the cost savings of the economics of scale.[12]

DIVESTITURE EXAMPLES FROM ANTITRUST APPLICATIONS

Not only the federal courts but the federal commissions have dealt with divestiture in antitrust cases. The Federal Trade Commission found that the Procter & Gamble Company's acquisition of Clorox in 1963 would lessen competition in the household liquid bleach market. The FTC ordered a complete divestiture. The FTC applied earlier court opinions, particularly the 1957 Supreme Court decision involving the E. I. du Pont de Nemours & Company,[13] and rejected P&G's contention that the public interest would be protected by injunctive relief against increasing Clorox's dominance of the household liquid bleach market. The Commission decided that the competitive market environment could be corrected only by restoring the market to its premerger position. Complete divestiture of Clorox was ordered.[14]

One of the most frequently cited examples of court-ordered antitrust divestiture is the Supreme Court's decision on relief where the Court ordered the E. I. du Pont de Nemours & Company to divest its entire holdings of General Motors stock over a ten-year period. The Court said: "Complete divestiture is peculiarly appropriate in . . . acquisitions which violate Section 7 . . . The very words of Section 7 suggest that an undoing of the acquisition is a natural remedy."[15]

After-acquired assets may be included in the terms of a divestiture decree depending on the circumstances of whether the purposes of the decree to redress the violation and restore competition require it. In the case of an antitrust divestiture action against the Aluminum Company of America, the Supreme Court approved per curiam a district court decree requiring Alcoa to divest itself of a plant it had built after the illegal acquisition. The district court refused to accept Alcoa's argument that the plant was not an integral part of the original acquisition and hence was not necessary to reconstitute a viable competitor.[16]

Partial divestiture has been ordered by court action in selected cases. In the 1961 case against the Union Carbide Corporation, the Federal Trade Commission found that the acquisition of the Visking Corporation lessened the competition in the manufacture of polyethylene. The FTC ordered Union Carbide to divest Visking's polyethylene manufacturing business. The FTC noted that the choice of divestiture remedies is "to be exercised with the goal of restoring and ensuring the preservation of healthy competition in the relevant markets."[17] Partial divestiture was feasible because Visking was a strong competitor before the merger and maintained a viable organization after being separated from Union Carbide.[18]

A strong criticism has been raised against partial divestitures as an antitrust enforcement device. Ralph Nader's Study Group Report on Antitrust Enforcement pointed out this observation on partial divestitures in antitrust cases: "A no-divestiture order naturally raises eyebrows. But when a company divests itself of some of its acquisition, the record looks far more impressive. Beyond appearances, however, serious questions arise. Some partial divestitures begin to look like a more sophisticated version of the philosophy of everybody wins and nobody loses so evident in the no-divestiture cases."[19]

POSTMERGER DIVESTITURE STUDIES

Two studies on the effectiveness of divestiture orders in achieving antimerger relief have been conducted. The first was the 1969 Elzinga study, based on the dissertation Kenneth Elzinga completed at Michigan State.[20] He studied thirty-nine merger cases filed between 1950 and 1960, settled by either consent order or decided in the government's favor by the end of 1964. The cases were analyzed against a set of criteria and designated a success, sufficient, deficient, or unsuccessful. Successful was defined as a complete divestiture of the unlawfully acquired assets. An unsuccessful result was no divestiture or a divestiture to a nonviable firm. Sufficient and deficient orders contained a component of success but less than complete divestiture. Of the thirty-nine cases analyzed, there were only three successful cases and thirty-one unsuccessful ones. There were five cases rated sufficient or deficient. To remedy the problems of a low success rate and lengthy delays in divestiture, Elzinga recommended the following:

1. A presumption against partial divestiture because it consists of a "line of commerce" rather than the operations of a once-going business. It generally is not conducive to reestablishing a viable independent firm.

2. The government exercise greater supervision in the selection of a buyer for the divested assets because it is in the divesting firm's interest to seek out a buyer who will either be cooperative, phlegmatic in his or her rivalry, or destined to fail.

3. Not rely on injunctive provisions or bans on future acquisitions as a substitute for divestiture because the policing of such decrees is highly difficult and it is extremely difficult for the parties writing the decree to anticipate the natural evolution of the markets involved.[21]

The second study was conducted by M. Pfunder, D. Plaine, and A. M. Whittemore while students at the Yale Law School.[22]

The Yale study reviewed all 227 Section 7 cases after the 1950 amendments to the Clayton Act and terminated by January 1, 1970. Of the 227 cases, 137 cases (60 percent) resulted in divestiture. From the divestiture group, 114 cases were selected for further study. Information was complete enough on 103 cases for a detailed analysis. In eight cases, divestiture never occurred. In another ten cases, compliance occurred only after the final order was modified. As with the Elzinga study, the authors made three recommendations to improve the success rate in ordered divestitures. The recommendations were:

1. The entity ordered divested be required to be a complete economic package that is at least potentially profitable.
2. A buyer not be considered acceptable unless its purchase would dissipate the effects of the illegal acquisition.
3. Time limits in the decree should be strictly enforced and a divesting party be given no guarantee of a fair price for the divested assets.

Many of the recommendations made in the two studies have since been incorporated into the practices of both the Federal Trade Commission and the Department of Justice. Both agencies now insist on a veto power over the identity of the purchaser of the divested assets. Both agencies also have adopted tougher policies against modifying divestiture decrees to permit more time to complete the divestiture and both have been quicker to seek sanctions for noncompliance.[23]

During the Reagan administration, the Department of Justice and the FTC closed or settled four large merger cases pending before them. A ten-year-old antitrust suit against AT&T was settled with major divestitures of the operating companies. An even older case against IBM was dropped. A case against the eight largest U.S. oil companies was closed just before the trial was to begin. And an investigation of the four major American automobile companies was dropped. Theories based on corporate size as a measure and trends toward market concentrations were no longer acceptable for antitrust action.

Divestiture became an antitrust remedy to private litigants when two district court justices ordered divestiture in two vertical merger cases. In both cases, the plaintiff had been foreclosed as a supplier to the defendant. In the 1969 case of *Calnetics Corporation v. Volkswagen of America, Inc.*, Calnetics, a manufacturer of auto air conditioners suitable for use in Volkswagen automobiles, lost the Volkswagen contract when the car maker bought a competing supplier that by 1971 was supplying 71 percent of the market. The judge ordered complete divestiture.[24]

In a second case of *International Telephone & Telegraph Corporation v. General Telephone & Electronics Corporation*, ITT complained that GTE's horizontal telephone operating companies and vertical telephone equipment manufacturers acquisitions had foreclosed it as a supplier of telephone equipment to operating companies including GTE. The court agreed and decided that the "primary remedy" was the complete "divestiture of such of GTE's acquisitions as this court finds necessary to restore competition in the relevant market."[25]

DEPARTMENT OF JUSTICE MERGER GUIDELINES

In 1982 the Department of Justice published a set of merger guidelines that stated the substantive standards that would be applied in a premerger investigation to decide whether to challenge a proposed merger. The guidelines enabled the department, attorneys, and corporate officers to determine if an acquisition was feasible from the legal antitrust viewpoint. Questions and problem areas could then be worked out so that postmerger divestiture possibilities were greatly reduced. The result was that no company could consider undertaking a large acquisition without consulting its antitrust lawyers. Antitrust has changed from an angry and populist movement concentrating on trust-busting activity to one of a bureaucratically enforced set of legal rules. Antitrust's original concern was corporate size, but it has helped form a corporate viewpoint of unbounded growth. Successful corporations have learned to acquire unrelated firms in order to broaden their field of investment. These conglomerate mergers have no limit. Antitrust theory never developed an approach that would limit these mergers. Antitrust has encouraged the development of a managerial perspective that is consistent with unlimited corporate growth through unrelated mergers.[26]

ANTITRUST LAW IMPLEMENTATION

Based on the antitrust laws, implementation of the legal remedies when antitrust court action is required may include divestiture of a business segment. Divestiture was not designed as a penalty, but it was seen as a remedy to restore competition. Economic models have been developed to explain the social losses from monopoly situations. Because divestiture is an applied remedy to monopoly situations, several studies have questioned the effectiveness of divestiture implementation in antitrust cases. The Department of Justice tried to aid the complex implementation of divestiture by issuing a set of guidelines.

5

Divestitures in a Political Environment

Mergers and the associated divestitures operate in a political environment of power and wealth. Because business combinations have earned close government scrutiny, laws have been passed to control business combination activity and political pressures have been applied to enforce the laws in a manner favorable to those with political power.

Political environmental factors as they concern business acquisitions and divestitures include:

1. Mergers in the 1960s
2. Congressional reaction
3. Mergers as a career choice
4. New laws that affect the business environment
5. The hectic merger atmosphere
6. Politics and corporate restructuring
7. Securities laws that maintain some merger control

MERGERS IN THE 1960s

Mergers continued throughout the 1960s into the 1980s. The conglomerate mergers of the 1960s should not have been permitted considering the antitrust laws available. Peter Steiner claims that the conglomerate wave was at least partly due to the courts because "courts which traditionally interpreted securities laws to protect stockholders were reluctant to let these laws be used to stop mergers because such use might deprive stockholders of the opportunity to sell out at a premium."[1]

The leaders of these new conglomerate enterprises were not well liked in the business community. Their takeover methods were often unfriendly. "They did not operate their businesses; they manipulated reports. At best, they were financial wizards. At worst, they were snake oil salesmen or dream merchants riding the crest of a booming economy and soaring stock market, taking advantage of tax loopholes, gaps in accounting rules, and a gullible public."[2] In 1969 the stock market fell and the go-go years in conglomerate mergers were past. They were mostly affected by a dropping price earnings ratio (PE). Rumors abounded that conglomerates were not real business organizations.

CONGRESSIONAL REACTION

"Some conglomerates specialized in using adroit legal tricks to fatten their profits, and the example has been widely emulated."[3] Congress reacted with a series of laws to curtail the merger activity. The laws of the 1930s were extended by the Williams Act of 1968. The early securities laws required financial disclosure before a merger took place. The Williams Act was aimed at hostile corporate takeovers by requiring disclosure of information before a takeover was attempted. To the takeover artist, businesses appeared to be streams of future income to be bought and sold without reference to production technology, marketing channels, or any other unifying basis for operating a business.

MERGERS AS A CAREER CHOICE

Successful managers often were veterans of takeover battles. A career no longer depended on a successful product line. In 1980 *Business Week* reported that a Theodore Barry & Associates survey showed that "most executives have never participated in line management." The same article included another study by Korn Ferry International that indicated nearly one-half of the 1,700 corporate vice presidents surveyed began as financial or marketing executives rather than production officers.[4] In the 1970s the new industrial leaders, many of whom were educated in broad-based business schools, were familiar with case study analysis and less daunted by making unrelated mergers than their predecessors. Restrictive antitrust laws had developed to the point that potential merger partners had to be unrelated businesses.

If internal expansion was blocked, corporate earnings had to be invested somewhere. With periodic oil price increases, the world economy moved through a series of recessions and inflation. The results were a flat stock market price level. An inflation-eroded, dollar-value stock price provided an excellent opportunity for corporations with retained earnings to purchase undervalued assets in other corporations. The replacement value of these assets was increasing due to inflationary pressures that made the values appear even better. Bargain hunting on the corporate level became commonplace. As anyone knows who has participated in a department store "super sale," bargain hunting can be a vicious and potentially dangerous situation. However, a successful purchase can lead to great managerial satisfaction and be potentially very profitable. Corporate executive careers were frequently built on such success stories. Divestiture, mergers, and corporate structural remodeling became common. Soon many of the obvious bargains were purchased and purchase premiums of 50 to 75 percent were paid because of the need to continue the merger "feeding frenzy."

NEW LAWS THAT AFFECT THE BUSINESS ENVIRONMENT

To add to this situation, new laws controlled the advertisement of cigarettes on television in 1971 and the surgeon general's reports on the health effects of cigarette smoking were incentives for the cash-rich tobacco companies to invest their large earnings in nonrelated industries. In addition, Congress deregulated the finance, oil, bus, and airline industries during the Reagan administration. Some very large firms in these industries became bankrupt and targets for takeovers, mergers, and divestitures. With some corporations in a cash-rich situation while others were near bankruptcy, acquisitions, divestitures, and mergers were commonplace. Many of the bankruptcy-inspired mergers were unsuccessful and became later subjects for divestiture.

Railroad deregulation led to several megamergers. The Chessie System bought the Seaboard Coast Line in a 1980 transaction worth $1 billion to form the CSX Corporation. Union Pacific purchased the Missouri Pacific in 1982 for $900 million. In the same year, the Norfolk & Western combined with the Southern Railway in a $1.7 billion merger to form the Norfolk Southern Corporation. In 1983 the largest rail merger up to that time was completed. Santa Fe Industries merged with Southern Pacific to form a $2.3 billion corporation.

In 1980 railroad mergers were given a boost by the passing of the Staggers Rail Act that permitted the Interstate Commerce Commission to approve mergers if the "transportation benefits of consolidation outweigh the anti-competitive effects."[5] Since the act was passed, the ICC has allowed the rail lines to abandon uneconomic lines, to raise or lower fares, to compete with other forms of transportation, and to acquire trucking companies. The poor economics of short-haul rail freight were recognized and added another convincing reason to close branch rail lines. Large, merged railroads provided economical through freight routes. This type of combination was not available in the pre-1980s political atmosphere of strong antitrust activity, particularly when like-industry corporations merged.

THE HECTIC MERGER ATMOSPHERE

Mergers became "faddish." Many of these "shotgun" arrangements ended in divestitures. However, many of the divested segments were caught up in another acquisition, often purchased for the wrong economic reasons. The circle continued with another divestiture into another acquisition. No corporation was safe from the merger fever. There were hostile tender offers made by large firms with enormous financial resources. Many of the takeovers resulted in divested segments as the acquisition was assimilated. Defensive mergers competed with offensive mergers that added to the confusion in the corporate boardrooms. Cash offers increased from 32 percent of the 1969 mergers to 53 percent of the merger offers in 1979. Stock swaps were down from 60 percent in 1968 to 26 percent in 1979.[6] Cash offers were very difficult to resist.

Defensive acquisitions could rid a corporation of attractive cash reserves, thereby reducing the risk of an undesirable takeover. Sometimes acquisitions and mergers were put together in such haste that antitrust considerations were not reviewed. In some transactions, a "white knight" corporation stepped in to acquire a firm when it was trying to fight off a hostile takeover. Many of the problems of American business during the 1980s appeared self-inflicted.

POLITICS AND CORPORATE RESTRUCTURING

Since World War II, have national politics become a factor in corporate restructuring? In 1953, for example, President Eisenhower appointed Edward Howrey as chairman of the FTC. Howrey was a partner in the Washington legal firm of Sanders, Gravelle, Whitlock & Howrey before joining the Eisenhower administration. One of the partners, Whitlock, was the acting GOP chairman in charge of the National Committee, and the other partners' political connections were thought to be excellent. The law firm represented twenty-five to thirty corporations, many of whom had dealings with the FTC, including the Firestone Rubber Company, which had a case pending before the FTC.

Howrey began his tenure at the FTC with a wholesale purge of men who had opposed him on earlier cases. One of the FTC commissioners, Stephen Spingarn, claimed that the firings were politically motivated. Howrey then hired an FTC staff more closely attuned to his own thinking. Rather than depending on market share as an anticompetitive guideline, he required evidence of actual anticompetitive effects. He developed a revised set of "multiple factors" test to determine monopoly activity. *Business Week* commented on them: "Some observers say that as a practical matter, the FTC is setting standards of proof that

will make the lawyer's job almost impossible."[7] In 1955 Howrey was attacked for a sharp conflict of interest before he re-
signed to return to private practice. He claimed he had accomplished his goal of restructuring the FTC. In 1958 during the
investigation of the Sherman Adams/Industrialist Bernard
Goldfine scandal, it was discovered that Howrey had sent a
memo to Adams in 1953 describing the progress of the FTC
case against a Goldfine-controlled company, Northfield Mills.
After the memo was sent, the FTC settled the case by accepting
the written promise from Northfield management to describe
the contents of its manufactured goods, which it had not done
before the FTC case was filed. The FTC continued to receive
complaints about Northfield Mills goods' contents. In 1955
Goldfine asked Adams to make him an appointment with
Howrey about not filing suit against the Northfield Mills. The
FTC staff recommended the issuance of a formal complaint and
the forwarding of the case to the Justice Department for crimi-
nal prosecution. In 1957 there was another settlement similar
to the first.[8]

Appointments to the Federal Trade Commission are made
with political affiliation and power in mind. The entire history
of the FTC includes situations that can only be explained by
referring to their political impact.

Congress and direct intervention by the Executive Branch's
Department of Justice are not exempt from cases of political
overtones. In the early 1950s a lower staff level of the Antitrust
Division of the Department of Justice was investigating a possible monopoly suit against the *Kansas City Star*. However, the
investigation received little attention at the higher levels of the
division until orders were suddenly sent to file suit against the
newspaper. President Truman had personally ordered the suit
filed. The *Star* was a constant critic of the Truman administration's policies.[9]

In 1966 the West Coast–based Broadway-Hale department
store chain, the sixteenth largest, had purchased 30 percent of
the San Francisco Bay area store chain, Emporium Capwell,
which had sales of $166 million. FTC attorneys thought they
had a strong case to stop further purchasing of the stock and a
possible divestiture of current holdings. They recommended that

any settlement without divestiture be rejected. Attorneys for Broadway-Hale argued that not settling the case and insisting on a trial would reflect unfavorably on similar earlier case settlements. The earlier settlements would appear as political settlements. Under mounting political pressure and a promise from Broadway-Hale that the stock purchase was just an investment and not for control, the case was settled over the strong objections of the FTC staff. Later purchases by Broadway-Hale of the Meier and Frank Stores in Portland, Oregon, G. Fox in Hartford, Connecticut, and in 1968 Neiman-Marcus of Texas were approved after political favoritism was claimed in the media. In 1971 they purchased Bergdorf-Goodman in New York. Bergdorf's attorneys were edgy enough about the FTC ruling that they rewrote the merger announcement forty-five times before they would approve it for release.[10] All of these acquisitions were after Broadway-Hale executives claimed to the FTC that internal expansion doesn't occur in the department store field.

SECURITIES LAWS THAT MAINTAIN SOME MERGER CONTROL

Besides filing with the FTC on premerger activities, the Securities and Exchange Commission requires an acquiring company, if it issues securities, to register the shares by filing a registration statement. It often is a lengthy and elaborate document, although sometimes some of the information can be incorporated by reference to previously filed documents. Target companies with registered securities must use a proxy statement or information statement that complies with the regulations controlling annual shareholders' meetings. With unregistered shares at the target company, the target company will make sure there is adequate disclosure to avoid the violation of the fraud section of the securities laws. If the basic securities registration is followed, there should be little trouble with the acquisition from the Securities and Exchange Commission.

Under the Hat-Scott-Rodino Antitrust Improvements Act, the parties participating in the acquisition must file information on the businesses involved and the proposed acquisition. The information is used by the Federal Trade Commission and Antitrust Division of the Department of Justice. The government regulators will have time, at least thirty days, to evaluate a proposed acquisition and to determine if it should be challenged. The law is complicated and the filing complex. In general, the filing is required when:

The seller has annual sales or assets of at least $10 million and the buyer has sales or assets of at least $100 million or vice versa; and

After the acquisition the buyer holds 15 percent of the outstanding securities or assets of the seller or the buyer's interest in the seller's securities or assets is valued at $15 million or more.[11]

Since favorable tax treatment is usually a consideration of any acquisition, the securing of a favorable tax ruling from the Internal Revenue Service is a frequent condition of the closing of most acquisitions. The most frequent request is for an IRS ruling that it is a tax-free reorganization. Any application requires extensive documentation to support the legal grounds of a tax-free transaction. The IRS usually takes several months to respond.

Occasionally the tax laws will be used by the government to direct corporate divestiture activity. In the 1989 case of Mobil Oil, the largest U.S. firm with installations remaining at that time in South Africa announced it was closing its South African operations by selling the $400 million petroleum refining and marketing operations to a South African company, General Mining Union Corporation, for $155 million. Mobil Oil was the last of the 170 major U.S. corporations in South Africa. Mobil's decision was prompted by a change in U.S. tax law that was intended to drive American companies out of South Africa. Since 1988, U.S. companies cannot deduct South African taxes on their U.S. corporate income tax calculations. The change would cost Mobil millions in lost tax deductions. This broke the company's resolve to stay in South Africa. Mobil chairman Murray said, "This was a difficult decision because we continue to believe that our presence and our actions have contributed greatly to economic and social progress for nonwhites in South Africa." The U.S. tax laws had been used to force a corporate divestiture to meet national political policies.

POLITICAL ENVIRONMENT SUMMATION

Conglomerate mergers in the 1960s were numerous despite the possibility of antitrust law violations. The new conglomerate leaders were viewed by some as financial manipulators, not businessmen. Congress reacted by passing the Williams Act that was designed to reduce hostile corporate takeovers by providing premerger financial information.

Business careers, particularly of those who graduated from an academic business program, often were built on the basis of surviving corporate takeover battles. Corporate bargain hunting was active because of the economic fluctuations present throughout the 1970s. New laws came into effect controlling cigarette advertising and the deregulation of several major industries.

Mergers became very popular including mergers as a defense against takeovers. Politics, although always present in business, became overt again in the antitrust activities of the politically appointed commissioners of the FTC. For example, U.S. presidents have intervened in several occurences into antitrust cases. The securities laws were able to maintain some control over business combination activity.

6

National Borders and Corporate Activity

When merger and business combinations move from the domestic to the international environment, national protectionism can have serious affects on corporate expansion and restructuring. International considerations include:

1. International corporate expansion
2. National sovereignty questions
3. International antitrust activities
4. The European Community

In the 1980s, trade level agreements between countries, such as the U.S.-Japanese automobile importation quotas, have forced foreign manufacturers to purchase or build plants in the United States. This has happened with Japan's automobile manufacturers.

INTERNATIONAL CORPORATE EXPANSION

Corporate expansion into the international business arena has continued to follow the pattern of acquisition in the host country, and if projected results do not occur, the divestiture of the acquisition. National pride is not injured as severely as when local products are forced out of the marketplace by imports with the foreign product name.

Matsushita Electric Company of Japan has been involved in overseas production of its electrical appliances and electronics. By the mid-1980s, the company was producing its products in 50 plants located in over 20 different countries, mostly in the developing Third World. However, trade friction had developed to imported electrical products in the developed nations. Matsushita decided to participate in the U.S. market by purchasing manufacturing facilities in the United States. In 1974 the company purchased a Motorola plant near Chicago that made television sets. It was refurbished to produce microwave ovens as well as TV sets for the home U.S. market under the Motorola trade name. In Tennessee a new Matsushita plant manufactures electronic components and electric fans. As an introduction of Japanese management practices into its U.S. plants, Matsushita executives invited key suppliers to its American plants to develop the close supplier-manufacturer relationships experienced in Japan. Up to this point, the Matsushita expansion plan has been very successful.

Midland Bank, the third largest United Kingdom bank in assets and fourth in capitalization, purchased the Crocker Banks, headquartered in San Francisco. Midland bought Crocker in two stages. The first was in 1980 when it purchased 57 percent of Crocker's outstanding shares, and the remaining 43 percent in 1985. Midland has been disappointed with the acquisition, but it was viewed as an inroad into U.S. financial investments. Midland has taken a more substantial role in management since Crocker's poor financial performance has continued. A potential divestiture situation is building if performance is not improved.

Nationalistic fervor can force this type of foreign ownership out of their investments. The copper companies in Chile, multiple types of investments in Iran, and foreign plants in the early portion of the Communist government takeover in mainland China are examples of forced divestiture by governments seizing corporate assets when political systems and attitudes change. In the case of South Africa, nationalistic fervor has forced divestiture of some South African operations of international corporations.

NATIONAL SOVEREIGNTY QUESTIONS

National sovereignty has limited the application of U.S. controls of transnational corporations. Foreign governments are very reluctant to permit the enforcement of U.S. business and particularly antitrust laws on companies incorporated in their country but operating in the United States. If the foreign company does not operate in the United States but has a direct influence on markets competed in by U.S. companies, U.S. securities and antitrust laws, of course, are unenforceable on the foreign operation. The foreign corporation has the market advantage in such cases. In the United Kingdom, the British government adopted legislation in the early 1980s that increases the powers of the British secretary of state to prevent compliance with certain types of foreign legal demands. Specifically, evidence or other orders that offend British jurisdiction or sovereignty will not be recognized. The law limits enforcement in Great Britain of foreign antitrust and multiple damage judgments, and enables British persons and companies to recover damages paid under foreign judgments in excess of actual damages to the foreign plaintiff.[1]

INTERNATIONAL ANTITRUST ACTIVITIES

The differences between nations concerning antitrust enforcement have made agreements in the antitrust field impossible. The 1979 Organization for Economic Cooperation and Development (OECD) Council Recommendation of Cooperation in Restrictive Business Practices Affecting International Trade calls for member states "to cooperate with foreign investigations where national laws and national interest permit." This procedure requires a case by case approach in resolving problems.[2]

Transnational mergers and joint ventures often raise similar problems. U.S. law enforcement has been slow to act in these cases because of comity considerations. Comity refers to social harmony concerns. Also affecting the applications of U.S. laws is the condition that Section 7 of the Clayton Act applies only to corporations engaged in domestic commerce, and does not apply when one is a foreign corporation. Differences in culture, business practices, and language add complications to the enforcement situation. The FTC opposed an acquisition by the J. I. Case Company of the French firm Poclain, one of Europe's largest manufacturers of heavy construction equipment. Poclain was in financial difficulty so Case, a division of Tenneco, offered to purchase a 40 percent interest in Poclain, which would assure its control of Poclain's U.S. assets. Both Case and Poclain produced hydraulic excavators and cranes, although Poclain had not sold its products in the United States. The French government approved the merger.

Considerations of comity, the importance of the merger to the French economy, and the low probability of a European company in serious financial condition entering the U.S. market were factors leading the FTC commissioners to approve the acquisition in spite of the staff's recommendation of disapproval.[3]

Because of these factors, comity, jurisdiction, additional barriers to market entry, and the difficulties of gathering evidence, U.S. antitrust laws dealing with economic concentrations have more impact on domestic corporations than foreign firms. It should be remembered, however, that U.S. firms can join with foreign companies and compete in foreign markets without any concern with U.S. antitrust laws. Some have suggested that antitrust activity in the foreign markets should be a matter of diplomacy rather than law. Most think it is unlikely to occur because of the significant changes required in both procedures and substance.[4]

THE EUROPEAN COMMUNITY

In the case of the European Community, the basic antitrust law is Articles 85 and 86 of the European Economic Community Treaty. Article 85 prohibits restrictive agreements. Article 86 prohibits the abuse of dominant market position by one or more firms. Both articles require an undesirable effect on trade between members of the European Community.[5]

Dominant positions are not themselves unlawful. It is the abuse of the dominant position that is prohibited, including any anticompetitive and exclusionary behavior. A monopoly does not have to prove its position legitimately, and no action can be taken to end the dominance, no matter how socially undesirable it may seem to do so. The theory of dominance can be applied to smaller corporations than generally affected under U.S. law.

Article 86 also contains a clause prohibiting abuse of a dominant position "in a substantial part" of the Common Market. Current and planned economic integration of the European Community may change the dominance application as a free flow of goods begins to cross national borders. With mergers and acquisitions of an European Community company, regional dominance also is a factor and its presence may prohibit the merger under Article 86.

NATIONAL BORDERS AND CORPORATE ACTIVITY SUMMATION

The presence of national borders and sovereignty raise significant questions in the rapidly expanding world of international trade. Corporations are international to an extent not seen before in the history of commerce. Corporate expansion on the international front has been based on mergers and acquisitions of national companies within the country of interest. Antitrust activities and anticompetitive behavior have been difficult to control because of the differing concepts of what anticompetitive behavior actually is, completely different bases for antitrust law, and the sovereignty limitations of information transfer.

In the European Community, the lowering of internal trade barriers and the agreement of European block countries has, on the surface, simplified antitrust considerations. However, the European community pact contains antitrust provisions that vary significantly from those in the U.S. and appear to be equally as difficult to apply within the European borders in an atmosphere of corporate acquisitions and expansion.

7

International Expansion
and Divestiture

Acquisitions of divested segments as well as entire entities have become normal business practices in the globalization of the world economy. The experience of U.S. companies making foreign acquisitions is relatively familiar. The foreign purchase of businesses including divested segments has become common practice in other countries as well as with U.S. companies acquiring overseas entities. The practice has been divided into:

1. Divestiture and acquisition as a means of international expansion
2. Jurisdictional disputes
3. Protectionism

INTERNATIONAL ACQUISITION AND DIVESTITURE

The acquisition of a business is a quick way to expand into a new business environment. The new situation may be a different culture, area, or economic sphere of influence. Internal development of new products in existing markets requires none of these sudden, dramatic economic challenges. As divestiture is a dramatic remedy to a business situation, a possible matching acquisition of the divested segment can be just as dramatic to the purchaser. When markets mature as they have in segments of most national markets, corporations may have no other choice than international expansion for rapid growth.

As the highly competitive marketplace for cement in Canada has grown, Lake Ontario Cement Limited has also grown by adding to its own capacity and acquiring other cement plants in both the United States and Canada. Well-financed European investors have purchased many other Canadian cement producers that were in financial difficulties. Lake Ontario Cement has tried to broaden its product base by acquiring seven companies that manufacture concrete and precast cement products. Its recent acquisitions in construction chemicals, sand, gravel and crushed stone have nearly completed its comprehensive product line based on a common technology.

In the case of Japanese industry where Matsushita Electric Company is the second largest Japanese electrical firm and the world's largest seller of electric appliances, the company has determined that the consumer electronics industry is mature. Management has decided to emphasize industrial electronics and office automation. As discussed in the prior chapter, Matsushita purchased a divested Motorola television plant near Chicago and produced microwave ovens and television sets.

Japan's largest pharmaceutical manufacturer, Takeda Chemical Industries, Ltd., has experienced the growing competition of foreign producers in the Japanese market. When Takeda management compared its international sales of 5 percent of total sales to the three leading Swiss drug companies' 90 percent overseas sales and the U.S. firms' 70 percent of sales, Takeda decided that the only answer was international expansion. With government controls on the price of drugs sold in Japan, the principal avenue for corporate growth would have to be in quantity. The two forces of domestic market competition and government product price controls contributed to the management decision to enter joint ventures, acquisitions, and new construction in foreign countries. Takeda became very active in the acquisition of divested corporate segments as an entree to foreign markets where they had not marketed a product.

A U.S. company, Hercules, Inc., has spent the period from 1977 through 1987 divesting its oil-based chemical products. Hercules management thought a large acquisition was the road to expansion. In 1988 Hercules management finished its decade of divestiture and decided to enter a series of joint ventures rather than the planned large acquisition. By selling the company's share of the commodity chemical firm, Himont Inc., in 1989, Hercules invested further in its Italian joint venture with BAT International S.r.1. The joint venture broke ground in 1989 for a Rome plant to make high technology composite including glass and steellike aramid fibers as well as carbon. In another related joint venture with Montedison S.p.A. of Italy, Hercules formed a joint venture to investigate shipbuilding applications to composite material.[1]

International joint ventures, however, have not all been successful. Differences in management outlook and expectations can contribute to the failure of an otherwise successful joint venture. U.S. executives often adopt a legalistic view by confining the joint venture's activities to those spelled out in the written document creating the venture. Japanese businessmen take a more organic view expecting the contractual agreement to change and evolve over time. The Japanese are more patient than their U.S. counterparts in permitting the joint venture to be successful. With the American business culture steeped in "success as quickly as possible," anything less than robust profitability is generally not sufficient for the U.S. partners. In the case of the Sin-Etsu Chemical and Dow Corning companies, their joint venture, SEH, manufactured silicon compound for semiconductor applications. After 12 years, sufficient profitability had not been reached according to Dow Corning officials, although the venture had experienced rapid growth. Possibly because of the growth rate, profits had been slow in keeping up. The resulting lower than acceptable return on investment led to the withdrawal of Dow Corning. Sin-Etsu purchased Dow Corning's divested share and continued with the rapidly growing silicon firm.

As a result of a rapid expansionary movement, a corporation can overextend itself. Barclays Bank PLC, Britain's second largest bank, planned on selling a portion of its U.S. retail branches. The bank wanted to concentrate on building its corporate business by focusing on service facilities for its worldwide clients rather than making a priority of putting funds into its retail operations. Approximately 135 Barclays branches in New York and California were closed. In the United States, Barclays presence was split between the East and West coasts and straddled the retail and corporate banking sectors. In 1986 Barclay lost its position as Britain's biggest and most profitable bank to National Westminster Bank PLC. Then in 1988, the bank implemented a major reorganization of its British operations that converted 300 of its 2,800 UK branches to specialized business centers serving principally business clients. The U.S. divestiture was a logical extension of the reorganization on an international scale. Profits of the sale were reinvested into developing business client centers in the remaining U.S. centers with some monies shifted to other international areas.[2]

In another case, the General Electric Company completed the 1988 divestiture of its consumer electronics business to French electronics giant Thomson S.A. in return for Thomson's medical equipment business and cash. Thomson plans to market TV sets and videocassette recorders in the United States under the GE and RCA names. The exchange for Thomson's medical equipment business, which had 1986 sales of $770 million, gave GE an entry into operations overseas where it had not presently operated. GE's worldwide hospital and laboratory diagnosis equipment was one of the company's fastest growing divisions with 1986 sales of $1.6 billion.[3]

JURISDICTIONAL DISPUTES

As the U.S. dollar weakens on the world market, U.S. firms find it more difficult to accumulate the large amounts of wealth or borrowing power to acquire the wealth necessary to purchase foreign assets as a dramatic entry into foreign markets. On the other hand, realignments of U.S. firms make divested segments easy buys for foreign companies generating profits in the higher valued foreign currency. European countries also have experienced the influx of foreign investors from Japan as their currencies weaken against the yen. Investments have been in the form of new construction, acquiring existing companies, and purchasing portions of existing but financially troubled European companies.

The French government has proposed new rules to control possible abuses of corporate takeovers and stock trades involved with acquisitions and divestitures. Pressure within France has grown for such rule changes ever since 1988 when a French government-owned company, Pechiney S.A., acquired a U.S. company. This resulted in cries of illegal insider-trading. The new rules would require investors to disclose their holdings in terms of voting rights rather than as a percentage of shares outstanding. Target companies would be permitted to defend themselves by increasing their capital after a tender offer was made. Stiffer fines would result from violations. The Commission on Operations of the Bourse will initiate legal suits in French courts on behalf of third parties damaged by such corporate actions. The Commission also will investigate and determine fines for stock market irregularities.[4]

When a corporation exercises its acquisition powers across national borders, jurisdictional disputes between national court systems often result if close attention is not given to the specific financial laws of the countries involved. In 1970 the U.S. State Department legal advisor John Stevenson said: "In the overwhelming majority of cases where problems of jurisdiction have risen they have not been the result of invalid exercises of jurisdiction but rather of two valid, conflicting exercises of jurisdiction."[5]

Even the definition of a corporate entity can enter into international jurisdictional disputes when large mergers, acquisitions, divestitures, or joint ventures are concerned. In 1975 the United States Justice Department objected to a proposed international joint venture between Pratt & Whitney of Canada and Rolls Royce of Britain to produce an executive jet engine for sale in the United States. Because Pratt & Whitney of Canada was a wholly owned subsidiary of United Technologies of the United States, the Justice Department chose to treat United Technologies as one corporate entity including its subsidiary Pratt & Whitney of Canada. This gave the United States a foundation to review the joint venture and rule against it on the basis of a preclusion of potential future competition between these giant jet engine manufacturing companies. The contrary ruling frustrated a significant and welcome investment in Canada.

Sometimes a joint venture between a private company and a

government is more difficult to divest than a unit jointly held between two private corporations. This may be particularly true if the corporation is foreign. In the case of W.R. Grace & Co., the corporation had been on an extensive program of divesting its agricultural chemical group. In 1988 Grace sold its Bartow, Florida, phosphate fertilizer operations to a Swiss and Moroccan investor group. The sale was completed with few complications. However, in the case of its Trinidad ammonia chemical complex, Grace expected the sale to take much longer because it owned the complex in conjunction in partnership with the Trinidad government.[6]

It is generally recognized that a sale of a business segment in a foreign country will require approval of the foreign government. It was no surprise to Texaco Inc. that its divestment of Texaco's West German operations to Rheinisch-Westfaelisches Elektrizitaetswerk AG for $1.23 billion would require West German government approval. The sales transaction was completed after it received the required approval from the West German Federal Cartel Office. The sale, however, did depend on government approval before it could be completed.[7]

Although a strictly international jurisdictional dispute was not present in the restructuring divestiture of the Allegis Corporation, its sale of the Westin Hotels & Resorts unit to the Robert M. Bass Group and the Japanese Aoki Corporation for $1.35 billion did require the approval of both the U.S. and Canadian governments. Both countries permission was required because some of the Westin hotels involved in the divestiture were located in the U.S. as well as several in Canada. Either country could have prevented the completion of the divestiture.[8]

Jurisdictional disputes can take many forms. For example, the purchase of a divested segment may jeopardize government-sponsored research. Sumitomo Heavy Industries Ltd. of Japan agreed to purchase Noranda's Lumonics Inc. unit for $70.6 million. Sumitomo's offer was conditional upon receiving assurances from the Canadian and British governments concerning Lumonic's continuing participation in government-backed research and development programs. The acquisition also was examined by a Canadian government agency, Investment Canada, to determine if it would produce a net benefit to Canada.[9]

In April 1989 the British government authorized the Anglo-German purchase of Plessey, a British defense contractor. The government purchase authorization of West Germany's Siemens AG and Britain's General Electric Co. PLC was one of the first foreign takeovers signaling a new era of foreign acquisitions in England. The required conditions did include a British partner and significant steps to safeguard classified information. American and continental defense contractors were then free to form British links.

Although national barriers are difficult to overcome in business divestitures and related acquisitions, companies such as Plessey can become interested in further combinations. Plessey began to consider divesting its highly respected telecommunications holdings and combining some of its defense businesses with France's Thomson. The barriers were down for planning and implementing international business operations in a previously politically impossible area.[10]

In the United States, a similar situation has occurred. Encore Computer Corporation, a small U.S. super minicomputer maker seeking new markets, agreed to purchase the divested U.S. computer segment, Gould Computers of Japan's Nippon Mining Co. Because of its Japanese parent, Gould Computer was a distressed property in danger of not getting enough defense business. The acquisition, which alleviated this situation, was subject to approval of U.S. government regulatory agencies and the boards of the respective companies. Gould Computer had a 500-member sales staff in Europe, which gave Encore access to the European market.[11]

PROTECTIONISM

When one corporation divests itself of a segment, acquisition by a foreign company may be excluded by protectionist overtones in recent government rulings. Protectionism need not be formalized by specific laws to be effective. Labelling agreements to restrict corporate acquisition activities as "voluntary" can be very effective in discouraging any future similar foreign acquisition attempts. Press stories publicizing the understanding that "authorities" would not permit foreign divestiture acquisitions may be unchallenged by legal action. In a 1985 study a British banker stated that there was a common, unwritten understanding that "the authorities" would not permit a foreign bank to gain control of a major United Kingdom bank.[12]

Germany's Siemens A.G. discovered protectionism and the residual of the anti-Nazi feelings after World War II. When the company tried to expand its markets in England, France, and the United States, and then their offices and manufacturing facilities, they were prohibited from dealing with electronic components, nuclear energy, or data processing until the late 1950s. Since that time, Siemens has been permitted to acquire and expand its own facilities and products in western Europe and the United States. Siemens is a major supplier of office and factory automation, telecommunications, and computer components. Siemens now can acquire, make competitive bids, and divest segments if necessary in all Western countries in which it sells products or services.

In 1984 Kenichi Ohmae, head of McKinsey & Company's Japanese practice, thought it advantageous for any company seeking to develop a market in a foreign country to form a loose corporate alliance, which he calls an "international consortia." The consortia allows traditional competitors to share distribution resources without conflicting with each individual company in the marketplace. For example, Burroughs includes Fujitsu's high-speed printer in its package of office automation products. Burroughs also manufactures Nippon Electric's optical character-reading equipment. Toshiba's high-speed facsimile printers are distributed in the United States by Telautograph and Pitney Bowes and in Europe by ITT. Ohmae thought it necessary to become an insider by forming an international consortia in the triad of Europe, Japan, and the United States.

Being an insider is necessary because:

1. Technology is advancing so rapidly that life cycles for some products have been squeezed into a matter of months.
2. It is necessary to keep up with changing tastes.
3. Only insiders have immunity against protectionist measures.
4. Domestic markets, including Japan and the United States, are too

small to absorb the output of world class automated plants needed for economies of scale in many product areas.[13]

Another practice to dull the impact of possible protectionism is the use of multinational executives from all countries involved in the corporation's operations. The Italian company, Montedison, has established such a practice. Several of the major executives are Americans. They have hired some English, Dutch, and German managers and some Italians with international experience. According to the company president, Mario Schieberni, "The American managers were generally more profit-oriented than Europeans and more competitive. The Americans love a challenge. I have managed the cultural mix consciously, putting Americans at the holding company level or in staff positions and Germans at the operating levels, because these two cultures did not work well together and Americans worked better with Italians. I also used mostly Italians in the negotiations with the government."[14]

In 1988 the U.S. Federal Reserve Board required all member banks to keep on hand twice as much capital in reserve for non-U.S. mortgages than overseas banks operating in the United States. U.S. banks with foreign investments in foreign mortgages were put at a competitive corporate disadvantage to foreign banks. As a result of this and the need to raise capital for more profitable operations, Chemical Bank announced that it was putting its $2.38-billion British home-mortgage business up for sale. The British home-mortgage business is profitable, but it doesn't meet the corporation's long-term strategy. The sale would complete Chemical's plan to dispose of lower margin retail operations outside the United States so that management could concentrate on the more profitable international trading and fund management businesses. Prior to the 1988 sale, Chemical had put its $1.3 billion consumer finance business up for sale, but later withdrew it after not finding a buyer. Both a factoring and a data processing unit have sold. Staff reductions had already begun in Britain. Discrimination against a U.S. company by the U.S. government for overseas operations is a case of protectionism by stressing the value of U.S. companies remaining at home for business operations.[15]

National security considerations become a protectionism factor when divestiture or acquisition of defense contractors is involved. The 1988 U.S. foreign trade bill strengthened the power of the Defense Department in citing national security implications to question or block acquisitions of U.S. businesses by foreign companies. During the first quarter of 1989, the Defense Department reviewed 35 proposed deals and the department was put under increasing political pressure to become more active in reviewing more merger cases.

When representatives of Britain's Consolidated Gold Fields PLC received a hostile takeover bid from South Africa's Minorco S.A. for $4 billion, Consolidated management persuaded the Secretary of Defense to order a top priority review of the takeover bid. The grounds for the order were Consolidated's U.S. titanium and gold mining operations, making it important to the federal government's strategic minerals policy. In response and to allay U.S. concerns, Minorco revised its bid by agreeing to spin off some U.S. assets. A U.S. district court judge issued an injunction against the takeover because the combined company would control 32.3 percent on the non-Communist world's gold market. Minorco withdrew its takeover bid. This was the first time that U.S. courts have stopped a merger between two foreign companies where the transaction is legal in the country with jurisdiction over acquisition. Other takeover target companies may imitate this defensive maneuver, especially as more European acquisitions involve companies with U.S assets.[16]

Other examples of Pentagon reviews are:

- The proposed acquisition of the manufacturing and research subsidiary of International Business Machine's Rolm division by West Germany's Siemens A.G.

- Cincinnati Milacron Inc.'s planned sale of a silicon wafer-producing unit to Osaka Titanium Co. Protection of the U.S. computer chip technology was the review basis.

- The planned acquisition of General Ceramics Inc. of Haskel, New Jersey, by Japan's Tokuyama Soda Company. The U.S. company produces specialized ceramics for military uses and it conducts classified nuclear research for the Oak Ridge National Laboratory.[17]

Protectionism presents itself in various forms. In 1987 U.S. entertainment industry executives were reported to be dismayed that CBS Records was considering selling its operations to the Japanese Sony Corporation. They pointed out that the 1986 sale of the third largest U.S. record company, RCA Records, was to West Germany's Bertelsmann AG. PolyGram Records and Capitol Records also are owned by Europeans. A major portion of the U.S. record production is owned by foreign investors. Bhaskar Menon, chairman of EMI Music Worldwide, a unit of Britain's Thorn-EMI PLC that includes Capitol Records, said the Sony purchase "puts the world record industry, in which American music plays such a very significant part, in a position where there is only one American record company of worldwide significance left." That company was Warner Communications Inc., whose record unit is CBS Records.

David Geffen of Geffen Records, which is distributed by Warner, said, "Since you can't manufacture American culture in Japan and Germany, I guess you have to buy it. Maybe they'll buy the movie studios next." U.S. record companies were particularly concerned by the purchase of the divested CBS record company because the industry has long maintained that the Japanese hardware manufacturers have no respect for copyright protection laws. Such laws are almost nonexistent in Japan. Now Sony will jump over the copyright protectionist laws and enter the U.S. and world markets as a significant participate in the record industry.[18] This is expected to add an incentive to other Japanese companies to search for acquisition opportunities.

Britain's Sir James Goldsmith bid $5 billion for Goodyear Tire & Rubber Co. in November, 1986, but withdrew his bid after making a greenmail profit on his 12.5 million shares. He withdrew his bid following threatening moves by the Ohio legislature to stop his purchase of Goodyear.[19]

One of the forces countering the pressures of protectionism was the need of cash-rich Japanese businesses to locate relatively safe and productive investments. Peter Rona, chief executive officer of IBJ-Schroder Bank & Trust Company, a unit of the Industrial Bank of Japan, stated, "The outlook for further Japanese acquisitions in the U.S. remains strong in light of the continuing very heavy capital requirements of the American economy and the very substantial surplus of Japan." In the case of the Japanese trading companies, they have to look beyond their borders because their traditional export business had slumped. Mitsubishi Corporation, the world's largest trading company, had taken such a position by stepping up its merger and acquisition activity in the U.S.[20]

Protectionism is not limited to the U.S. and Japan. Britain's Department of Trade and Industry blocked the proposed $2.76 billion takeover of Scottish & Newcastle Breweries PLC by Elders IXL Ltd., an Australian conglomerate. Industry Secretary Lord Young began a broad reform designed to make the British brewing industry more competitive. He said, "What we can't do is see monopoly situations created." The basis for the blockage of the takeover was that Elders already owns Courage, Britain's sixth largest brewer. After the ruling, John Elliot, chairman of Elders, said the company will "review the basis of the finding and determine an appropriate strategy for Europe."

A 501-page report by the Monopolies and Mergers Commission was critical of the brewing industry, attacking the long-standing arrangement by which breweries own or control pubs and limit the types of beer the pubs may sell. The commission recommended that breweries each be limited to ownership of 2,000 pubs, and that these be allowed to offer one guest beer produced by an unaffiliated brewery. The limit, which takes effect after 36 months, would require a wholesale divestiture of pubs by Britain's major breweries. Some of the breweries own more than 5,000 pubs. Some breweries may retain their pubs and sell their breweries.

In addition to Elders, Bass PLC, which has 20 percent of the British beer market, Grand Metropolitan PLC was expected to be disrupted by the ruling. Each had networks of pubs above the proposed threshold and would be forced to sell portions of them. Price increases were blamed on the lack of competition in the beer industry.[21]

INTERNATIONAL EXPANSION AND DIVESTITURE
SUMMATION

The frequent divestiture and acquisition methods for corporate restructuring has become popular in international commerce. Divestiture as a source of capital and the elimination of an unwanted business segment can lead to either an acquisition or a joint venture. In the foreign marketplace, such corporate activity may lead to jurisdictional disputes in the case of national commerce legal controls. This is particularly true in the case of antitrust and the possible complications of segment divestitures.

Protectionism may become the basis of governmental intervention in corporate divestitures and acquisitions. Foreign access to national security materials may result in the refusal of governmental approval for a business combination change.

8

Corporate Reactions

When the corporation experiences changes in the business environment, in the political atmosphere, or in nationalistic objectives, it can cope by exercising one or more of a number of managerial reactions.

The corporation may react in a number of ways such as:

1. Adding or reducing the number of products
2. Reducing costs
3. Research and development
4. Mergers and acquisitions
5. Strengthening the manufacturing or distribution system
6. Continuing as is
7. Shutting down
8. Divestiture

Unexpected poor company performance may be necessary to spur management to action, but a corporate turnaround in decline usually requires substantial changes in the business. Greater risk and uncertainty tend to be associated with undertakings yet to be assumed. The present return, no matter how poor, has the advantage of certainty with its apparent better definition of attendant risk. Management may explain the condition of the business as due to a short-term economic cycle. Changes in the corporation and the way it conducts its business, however, has long-term corporate effects and should be viewed from a position of long-term economic success. No business or industry is independent of national and regional economic changes. A systematic evaluation of the interdependency of the corporation and the economic cycle provides management with important information for long-term corporate decision making.

As management reviews the corporation's situation in today's profit conscious business environment, they may respond by focusing on the need to restructure the corporation. Restructuring means a basic change in the activities a business undertakes such as: the kind of businesses or industries it is engaged in, the products or services it offers, or the geographic areas served. Restructuring also may mean how a company conducts its business or a change made in the orientation of management policies. When management, the government, or some other outside influence decides the corporation needs to restructure, it may take the form of narrowing the corporate focus away from unpromising operations toward more rewarding activities. Strategic restructuring also may include the shedding of particular business segments.

As restructuring implies organizational changes, refocusing refers to a managerial attitudinal shift. As James Brown wrote in the Conference Board report, *Refocusing the Company's Business:* In refocusing "a company is compelled to broaden or shift its focus in the sense of enlarging its interests, entering businesses different from its present ones and reducing its relative commitment to the latter." The refocusing can include diversification as well as divestitures. But diversification has its problems as pointed out in the research report, "If diversification is undertaken, it should be confined to businesses with related strengths, skills or resources."[1] And, "Acquisition is a tough way to refocus. There are no 'pure' companies in any industry, so any acquisition is likely to cause a blur of corporate focus."[2] The author adds, "management may, therefore, deem it prudent to narrow the corporate focus by shedding less promising businesses and concentrate on the more promising ones."[3]

Brown comments on some contributors' thoughts about what it takes within a company to really be considered as refocusing the business. Their thoughts were, "a company has refocused only if it makes a significant commitment, relative to its resources, to a change in its business mix."[4]

N. V. Philips, the leading European manufacturer of semiconductors, announced that it was restructuring its global operations in the integrated circuit business by 1990. The corporation will have two newly created business units for designated products. One will be located at Signetics Corp., Philips' Sunnyvale, California facility and the other will be based at corporate headquarters in Eindhoven, The Netherlands. Worldwide marketing and sales will be managed centrally from Eindhoven instead of locally. The restructuring is an attempt of Philips' management to focus on strengthening Philips' international position and possibly improving a weak sales and marketing organization in the integrated circuit industry.[5]

ADDING OR REDUCING THE NUMBER OF PRODUCTS

Management may react by adding a product to improve sales or profit performance. Often, without a thorough review of its position in the economy, corporate management may select a product based on knowledge developed during the growth portion of the corporate life cycle. Economic conditions may not be the same now. Reducing the product line also may be built on the same false premises. The problems that brought poor business performance may go far deeper than can be solved by changing the product mix.

REDUCING COSTS

When profit performance is inadequate, cut costs! Although this may be the easiest and most frequent solution, cost cutting often is a reaction reached in haste by a management not willing or able to consider other more effective remedies for a declining corporation. General management who have emerged from engineering, production, or accounting often see cost reduction as the answer whenever profits fall below desired levels. Other possible remedies may not be considered.

RESEARCH AND DEVELOPMENT

To maintain its economic position, the corporation has to either conduct product research or have access to the results of technological product research. In addition, a corporation must be willing to invest enough monies to implement technological change in product introduction, production, advertising, and distribution. Technological change can provide early warning signs for impending economic changes, far ahead of financial system warnings. Although such technological information is voluminous and sometimes difficult to apply to specific industries or products, it must be interpreted on a timely basis. A corporation that finds it is in an unfavorable research position must determine whether or not it wants to remain in the particular business. Research and development is a long-term process and generally does not react quickly enough to significantly help a business that has declined for a period of time.

MERGERS AND ACQUISITIONS

The answer for many corporations found in adverse economic conditions is to merge or acquire another, stronger company. A merger can create a true economic gain if the combination of the financial resources reduces the lender's risks compared to the individual firms. If the unmerged firms are individually financially sound and reasonably good financial risks, the reduction of financial risks due to a merger may be insignificant and therefore questionable.[6]

Corporations may merge to improve specific business operations. For example, Saudi Arabia and Venezuela have expressed a strong interest in gaining a direct access to foreign oil markets by acquiring refining and distribution operations including ones in the United States.[7] Japanese automobile manufacturers have formed joint ventures with U.S. auto makers to provide marketing outlets in exchange for the use of manufacturing facilities in Japan. Mergers and acquisitions are available to solve business situations if the weakness is identified and the merged entity is a significant solution to the actual problem. All too often a merger is arranged between two weak companies that form a larger weak company. These combinations merely delay the economic consequences of a declining corporate life cycle.

STRENGTHENING THE MANUFACTURING OR DISTRIBUTION SYSTEM

An alternative to adverse environmental conditions is to strengthen either the manufacturing or distribution systems. Whereas this alternative resembles cost cutting, strengthening a portion of the corporate activities may involve major infusions of capital over a period of time. Management reorganization, restructuring, and changes of key individuals in the particular operations also may be involved. The increased investment may have to be done under adverse conditions or seriously declining profits with investors clamoring for more immediate results than can be given with the partial corporate changes. The strengthening of manufacturing or distribution may be accomplished in combination with reductions in personnel, mergers, adding products, or any of the other actions that can be taken when a management finds the corporation in financial trouble.

CONTINUING AS IS

One alternative, of course, is the "Damn the torpedoes, full speed ahead!" approach. Although this is the material of heroic acts, it often is the business result of a paralyzed management that fails to make any decisions under extreme stress. When it is the chosen course of action, it indicates strong support for past decisions and management, and, of course, hopes they were sound decisions.

Compulsive restructuring can sap management's stick-to-itiveness when, in reality, perserverance would probably pay big dividends. Sidney Schoeffler, president of the Strategic Planning Institute, has conducted studies showing that "many companies make radical moves out of a business hastily and prematurely—when they haven't fully exhausted the cash or profit potentials of that business." He estimates that the average business fails to realize half its potential, and that means that "many managements would be far better off concentrating on managing what they have than looking for greener pastures."[8]

Confidence is a necessary ingredient for success in any endeavor. If it is the result of a decision process that has reasonably weighed the alternatives, "continue as is" may be the best strategic course of action. If management has diagnosed the economic future environment correctly. As with all projections, only time will tell if the decision was correct.

SHUTTING DOWN

Shutting down a plant or operation is extremely traumatic for both the management and the employees involved. As L. Vignola put it, "Quitting is probably the least attractive of the responses conceptually. To do something is at least psychologically reassuring; it is in the great American management tradition of action. But to shut down, to quit would seem to be the most bleak admission of failure."[9] K. R. Harrigan pointed out another aspect of management's reluctance to shut down an operation when he wrote, "Managerial reticence to shut down plants may be based on concerns for face-saving or sorrow for the welfare of the bulk of an isolated community that will be left jobless."[10]

Harrigan discussed a "planned liquidation" as an acronym for a shutdown. He commented that labor contracts must be settled, customers must be persuaded to substitute other products, and the monies expended to position the corporation in the competitive marketplace may be lost. Planned liquidations often are avoided because they represent shattered dreams, loss of jobs, confusion among suppliers and customers, and endless hassles over details. The manager who evaluated the situation and recommended a shutdown should be protected from internal or external retaliation because he unearthed the poorly performing unit and brought it to the attention of management.[11]

Of course, many corporations have closed production operations when financial conditions required it. For example, Olin permanently shut down chemical facilities that had been placed on standby because of deteriorating market conditions for the plant's output. Brown Shoe closed domestic shoe manufacturing plants in Kentucky and Missouri to consolidate their operations in other Missouri facilities. Local employees may be given opportunities to transfer to operating plants if openings exist for their particular skill. Often workers cannot or will not move from long-established homes. The damage to corporate goodwill is difficult to measure, but it usually is isolated to the affected community.

Another series of plant shutdowns by one corporation was tied to a major restructuring of the parent. Interco, Inc., composed of the four divisions of apparel, shoes, furniture, and retail operations, had turned away a number of hostile takeovers and was experiencing internal management turmoil as the divestiture of major divisions was evaluated. In 1986 Interco began to close selected midwestern Florsheim Shoe Division plants. The Poplar Bluff, Missouri, plant was preceded in 1984 by the closing of another Interco International Hat factory a short distance away in Oran, Missouri. In 1988 the corporate plant closings increased as they closed the International Shoe location in Perryville, Missouri, and the Florsheim Division in Jackson, Missouri. In 1989 closings continued in the Hat Division facilities at Dexter and Marble Hill, Missouri. All six plants were located within a 60-mile radius of each other in an area with little other industrialization. A plant spokesman was quoted as saying, "The closing (1989 in Dexter, MO) relates to corporate restructuring that the company is undergoing." Another spokesman stated, "Right now the company is concentrating on divesting its apparel division."

The need to close plants and divest operations wherever the corporation can find a buyer was blamed on shoe and textile imports from Taiwan, Spain, and Brazil. The employment impact on the local communities was serious. The jobs lost are shown in Table 8.1.

Over 2,800 jobs lost in a small area of southeast Missouri and northwest Kentucky from one company's plant closing is a sig-

Table 8.1

	Interco Division	Location	Jobs Lost
1975	Shoe	Sikeston, MO	450
1979	Shoe	Chaffee, MO	450
1986	Shoe	Poplar Bluff, MO	200
	Hat	Oran, MO	114
1988	Shoe	Jackson, MO	200
	Shoe	Marshall, MO	350
	Shoe	Cape Girardeau, MO	45
1989	Shoe	Hermann, MO	250
	Shoe	Paducah, KY	350
	Hat	Dexter, MO	200
	Hat	Marble Hill, MO	200
		Total Jobs Lost	2,809

nificant group of events due to a corporation participating in a strategic redirection. In 1988 legislation was introduced in the Congress to stabilize employment of the shoe, textile, and apparel industries. However, it passed the House vote but failed in the Senate. The economic impact of these closings in small towns was summarized by several workers given notice of the closing in the plant where they were employed.

This has not hit home yet with everybody. There were rumors going around so it was not a surprise to us.

People are worried about where they are going to find another job. Some people are bitter.

It is limited here. You either saw trees or sew hats. That is what has held this community together.

Any time a community in an area loses 200 workers, it will have an effect on the entire area. In many cases, a double burden occurs when both husband and wife are employed in the same factory.

This layoff is going to hurt the economy of this community. It is going to cut the throats of some small businesses. There is nothing else for these people to do.[12]

DIVESTITURE

An alternative often overlooked prior to the early 1970s is the divestiture of the unacceptable plant, division, or unit. A divestiture doesn't just happen. It is usually the result of years of struggling with an unfavorable situation and the failure of other corrective strategies. I. M. Duhaime and J. H. Grant found that divestiture decisions result most often from a complex interaction of influencing factors, seldom from the individual influences of single factors.[13] To make matters even more complex, S. C. Gilmour added that divestiture decisions are difficult and painful decisions for which hard analytical decision support was either unavailable or unused.[14] Divestiture can be rationalized on the basis that it will transfer remaining assets to a higher valued use or to a more efficient user. Another view is that a divestiture may enhance a firm's value by slicing off a business that is a poor fit with the remaining businesses. If these theories are valid, good divestiture programs may increase the market values of both the divesting and the purchasing corporations.[15]

Although there is a negative connotation with some businesspersons when the term "divestiture" is used, it has become an accepted strategic possibility. As alternatives are being weighed, the major determinants to a divestiture possibility are: unit strength, unit interdependency, and firm financial strength relative to industry averages. Comparisons to competitors are a very important influence on divestiture decisions.[16] If a company has attained a successful return on investment by being a superb marketing or R & D firm, its managers will encounter particularly difficult internal resistance to divesting businesses that are close to the heart of their corporate image.

When a unit was chosen for divestiture, a potential buyer would look at the return on investment (ROI) to the seller and then a ROI to the buyer, often on a leveraged basis to increase the ROI to an acceptable level. The removal of allocated corporate overhead and corporate transfer pricing policies also may increase the unit ROI in the buyer's evaluation. Some potential divestiture candidates may have an adequate return on investment, but the unit may not fit the strategic plans of the selling corporation. The critical issues in any divestiture evaluation revolve around the expected cash flow and a determination of vulnerabilities.[17]

Ramada Inc. signed an agreement to sell its Marie Callender Pie Shops Inc. unit to a company formed by closely held Hayes Financial Corp. and Hampton Ventures Inc. of New York. The sale was a portion of Ramada's restructuring from a hotel, restaurant, and casino company to a pure gambling concern. The Callender chain, purchased in 1986 for $81 million, expanded to 152 restaurants in 17 states, but encountered marketing problems and fierce competition. For the first nine months of 1988, Callender operating profit was $3.3 million compared to $7 million in a comparable period in 1987. Revenue also dropped. Completion of the Marie Callender sale and the remaining hotels will leave the corporation with the casinos management wants to operate.[18]

Sometimes divestitures are viewed as plant shutdowns. When AT&T received the federal court's Modification of Final Judgment, the order was to divest the local portions of its 22 Bell operating companies, thereby separating local exchange operations from the other parts of the business. AT&T's first task was to reduce its general department staff from nearly 13,000 to less than 2,000. As the corporate staff saw the divestiture order, it looked like a "plant shutdown."[19]

REACTION SUMMATION

When the business environment changes, the corporation can react by: adding or reducing the number of products, reducing costs, changing the research and development effort, arranging for a merger or acquisition, strengthening the internal manufacturing or distribution system, continuing as is, shutting down operations, or divesting a business segment. The alternatives require evaluation before a management selection can be made.

9

Divestiture Decisions

In many business life cycles, situations appear when divestiture becomes a viable alternative. Some of the frequent occurances that may lead to divestiture are:

1. Divestiture indicators
2. Recognition of managerial error
3. Acquisition fallout

During the last decade, corporate executives have developed strategic divestiture plans to eliminate unsuccessful sections of the business, rather than just spinning off an occasional unprofitable segment. If profits or the returns on invested capital were not as high as management, the stock market, or stockholders thought they should be, then action had to be taken. Divestiture is resisted by some managements because it may be interpreted as: admitting failure, the possibility of absorbing high losses in one accounting period, the fear of employee morale problems, and the latent fear that someone else may purchase a divested segment and turn it into a success. Such an embarrassment would not be risked by many managers.

When management decides to minimize the decision trauma as a business segment's profits slide below acceptable limits, management may be choosing a course that will not maximize the potential profits of divesting the segment. A general stigma to divestiture may be more extensive than a management embarrassment. Harowitz and Halliday in *The Journal of Business Strategy* mentioned that it is rare to see any reference in the literature to selling business units as a money making tactic. Businesses and businesspersons exist to grow bigger, not to shrink. Besides it's more fun to grow than to retrench! Weston told about the importance of growth to a corporation when he said:

Without growth possibilities, most firms would lose their purposes for existing, stagnate, wither, and then die. For the soundly operated firm, restructuring and realignments frequently are necessary adjuncts of growth—either to expand the firm as a whole, or, in many cases, to cut back the overall size of the company so that emphasis can be placed on the business segments with the best growth prospects.[1]

Another complication arises when it is realized that every corporate division (exceptions are very rare) is associated with at least one senior corporate officer whose personal reputation may be perceived to be soiled if his particular division is divested. If a division is for sale, doesn't that mean it is in trouble or in a declining industry? The knee jerk reaction is "Who would want to buy it anyway?" Managers with such attitudes dislike losers and through association, divestitures.[2]

General Electric's CEO John Welch, Jr., took a steel-fisted approach to divestiture. GE's core industries would go head-to-head with the Japanese on a global scale, but technology and services, protected from foreign competition by the nature of their business, would become the new General Electric. All other parts of the company, including small appliances and consumer electronics, were left to sink or swim on their own. If a division could not be made profitable, it was to be folded or sold. Welch wanted each business to be either first or second in its industry, or to have a shot at getting there.[3]

DIVESTITURE INDICATORS

Divestiture becomes an alternative when any of the following occurances exist in a multisegment corporation:

1. Unsatisfactory segment profit performance as determined by corporate management.

2. A desire to improve a corporate current or future cash flow position.

3. Avoidance of segment capital investment.

4. Corporate debt reduction.

5. A desire to reduce business risk.

6. High cost and badly located segment operations.

7. Desire for diversification hampered by being in a particular business.

8. Lack of segment fit with the other perceived activities of the corporation.

9. Lack of top management know-how in a particular business.

10. Personality conflicts among management, either at the segment level or with corporate management.

11. Receipt of an attractive segment offer.

12. Government decree to divest a business.

Divestiture decision making might involve just one problem in the mind of a key management person. Divestiture may become the single preferred alternative to which management commits from the outset. Alternatives may not even be considered.[4] With the process of such a single outcome calculation, decision makers will focus on divestiture of the unit, inferring positive outcomes for it and negative outcomes for all other alternatives. This may help reduce managerial stress from dealing with multiple alternatives for the unit.[5]

A survey reported in Vignola's book, *Strategic Divestment*, provided the reasons a sample of corporate managers gave for divesting a business segment.[6] Their responses are given as percentage of the total number of responses.

Poor performance	26%
Changes in plans	23%
Excessive resource needs	19%
Constraints in operations	15%

Source of funds	10%
Antitrust	7%
	———
Total	100%

As Lester Thurow said in his article "The Productivity Problem": "Disinvestment, or getting out of old sunset industries, is just as important a source of growth as getting into new sunrise industries."[7]

RECOGNITION OF MANAGERIAL ERROR

Corporate management is basically a risk business. Whenever there are human decisions, there is a risk of failure. With most people, there is a tendency to suppress the admission of failure. Divestitures are usually handled as a "family embarrassment." Most companies don't realize the maximum return from their divestments because of the hush-hush way they are dealt with when they have been identified. Divestment of inappropriate businesses is in many cases the foundation stone of a good strategy.[8] As Thackray sees it, "even incomplete or partially botched restructurings tend to be better than the corporate malaise they were meant to cure."[9]

In 1982 R. Tomasko of Arthur D. Little & Co. said, "Continental Can Co. and Champion International Corp. have done much better by sticking to core competences than American Can Co. Institutional investors need to assign higher risks to companies attempting big investments far from their root competence."[10]

Lucky Stores was a diversified major corporation that was built on a reputation of being the first discount supermarket organization. Acquisitions accounted for the rapid expansion. The management purchased restaurants, drug stores, women's wear, auto supply, and general discount stores. In 1983 the CEO of Lucky Stores was quoted as saying, "We realized we can't do everything well." By 1985, when it was a $9.2 billion sales corporation that ranked eighth among retailers and fourth among supermarket chains, security analysts were saying, "Lucky is a perfect example of a good retailer that tried diversification and failed." Another analyst said, "Lucky let the competition take over its prime markets." Lucky management responded by divesting its 240 store women's apparel business, 77 retail parts stores, and its 17 Eagle supermarkets.[11]

Du Pont spent years of research and development work and millions of dollars to develop Corfam to meet a needed improvement in shoe materials. However, performance fell far short of the minimum requirements. Du Pont recognized the failure of the product and divested much of the operation.

Sweden's Telefon AB L. M. Ericsson divested its troubled data systems division to Finland's Oy Nokia. Ericsson began its ill-fated venture into data products in 1981 when they hoped to create a powerful combination of telecommunications and computer technology. The company fell down in executing its strategy by fielding more products and opening worldwide sales offices than its slow-growing computer division could support. The losses grew to the level that Ericsson had to infuse cash into the division to keep it liquid. Company officials recognized that their strategy was flawed. "The idea was right at the time, but time has changed and we can see now that the situation is not the same," said Stig Larsson, information services division president. By selling the division in 1988, the company was free to concentrate on its telecommunications, cables and defense business.[12] Management recognized they had made an error.

Anyone can make an error. Avon has become a giant in the cosmetics business by making wise business decisions. However, their 1988 planned sale of the home health care unit, although recognized by security analysts as financially good for the company, was also said by the same analysts that "it doesn't make them look like the smartest guys in the world."[13]

Because there is less fear of disapproval today, divesting may be chosen as the remedy for operating situations that are marginally profitable.

ACQUISITION FALLOUT

Merger, acquisitions, and divestiture should be closely related. The research of C. J. Clarke and F. Gall showed that over 50 percent of all acquisitions fail to achieve the objectives of the acquisition.[14] Many of these acquisitions are later divested. The concept of acquisitions synergies has been found to be very difficult to realize in actual practice. Diversifying into a related field is likely to yield more synergism than pure conglomeration of highly unrelated diversification. The management is familiar with the markets or technology of the related business. Related field acquisitions do not provide the units for divestiture that unrelated diversifications provide.

Acquisitions may be completed for the wrong reasons. According to M. S. Salter and W. A. Weinhold, "There exists no economically based theory to justify wide-ranging corporate diversification. In fact, a strict reading of classical microeconomic theory (especially the concept of specialization) implies that by spreading resources among several businesses, corporate diversification can lead to lower profitability and reduced competitive strength."[15] However, A. Michel and I. Shaked conducted a study with opposite results than anticipated from the Salter and Weinhold comments. Their analysis indicated that if a corporation can stay together after an unrelated merger, it has a higher probability of producing a superior financial performance over those businesses that are predominantly related.[16] Often the CEO of the acquiring company may see an acquisition as image building because it appears as progressive, expansive, and exciting in the merger-minded business environment.

After the acquisition or merger, acquired business segments may be ill-fitting and underperforming mistakes that are retained far beyond the time they should be divested. The retention of some segments continues to weaken the overall corporate performance because the alternative that may come to mind, divestitures, is still viewed as negative and an admission of failure by some businesspersons. Management should be expected to make a percentage of poor business judgments, but they should also be expected to identify these mistakes or mismatches and remedy them by corrective action, which may include divestiture. To do otherwise would continue to lower the corporate performance.

A business activity not particularly wanted by the acquiring company may be included in the total acquisition. The exact or

even close matching internal capabilities of the acquiring com-
any with matching opportunities in the acquired organization
is often not attainable. The undesired entity flounders until the
new management recognizes the nonfit in the combined corporation and either provides the changes and support to make
the segment successful or prepares to divest it. In either case,
the acquiring company may keep only the "bright stars" of the
acquisition. When Campeau Corporation acquired the Federated Department Stores Inc. in the early months of 1988, Campeau executives had to spend $6.6 billion for Federated's shares,
$200 to $250 million in fees, assumption of about $800 million
in debt and bank loans. By April 1988 Campeau management
had told the press that they intended to sell $4.4 billion in Fed-
erated assets to help finance the acquisition. Federated's Gold
Circle and Wal-Mart discount stores were expected to be in the
multibillion-dollar sale.[17] In the case of Primark Corporation,
management's proposal to divest its Michigan Consolidated Gas
Co. in 1988 and return to unregulated communications and information service businesses had been anticipated by its chairman and chief executive officer. He was quoted as saying, "I
always knew the company had to be separated sometime. We
wanted to find a way to increase the value for shareholders
and to draw a distinction between our utility and diversified
units. I thought this was the right time."[18]

Acquisitions cause problems with the acquired executives.
According to R. M. Kanter and T. K. Seggerman, nearly half
the senior executives of an acquired firm leave within one year
of the acquisition and 75 percent will leave within three years.
These results came from a study of 150 large mergers and acquisitions conducted by the executive recruiting firm Lamallie
Associates. This may help explain why one-half to three-quar-
ters of all mergers and acquisitions eventually fail.[19]

Occasionally, an acquired segment is determined to be "too
small" in relationship to the parent corporation. Although it
may be profitable, the small division may not warrant the
amount of management or cash necessary to continue its success. Such small, desirable divisions may be easily and profitably sold with a minimum of disruption within the entire corporation.[20]

Another acquisition conflict that may result in divestiture is the merging of two disparate corporate cultures and value systems. When the differences are extreme and cannot be reconciled, a divestiture may be necessary, although it may cause high levels of uncertainty and anxiety among the management and employees of both merger partners. Divestiture of a merged segment may be the most practical solution available.

The business environment may unfavorably change between the time an acquisition is analyzed and agreed upon and its completion. For example, Avery Inc. purchased Uniroyal Chemical's specialty chemical company in 1987 but placed the chemical company up for sale in 1988. Avery tried to quickly build the purchased subsidiary into a large multinational chemical company through further acquisitions. However, price earnings multiples of other companies in the chemical industry rose, which frustrated Avery's search for acquisitions at acceptable prices. Earnings of the specialty chemical company were just sufficient to cover the interest expenses of the borrowed funds to purchase and build the company. Avery decided that the specialty chemical acquisition should be sold. Management placed it for sale.[21]

REASONS SUMMATION

Divestiture is recognized as a necessary managerial remedy when business situations arise that can best be solved by divesting a segment. Although there are common indicators pointing to divestiture solutions, managerial and economic judgment is required. When management indicates it made an error of judgment in a prior business decision, divestiture may be the specific solution required. Divestiture has become a frequent managerial method to realign corporations after a merger or acquisition.

10

Divestiture as
a Positive Solution

Divestiture generally is considered a negative business activity. The business is decreasing in size, which in the American culture is not desirable. Ferenbach commented on the desirability of divestiture as a business alternative when he said, "Often, in the case of divestitures, management is released from a bureaucratic environment where senior corporate managers do not understand the opportunities in the subsidiary business or are required to divert capital to other opportunities."[1]

When divestiture is the alternative chosen by the corporation to solve the present or potential financial problem, divestiture becomes a positive solution to help the corporation regain or improve its financial health. A divestiture may result in better managerial decision making and greater management incentive to succeed because of the reduced managerial span of control over operations. The operational effects of decisions made by a lower or midlevel manager can be detected easier in a smaller organization than it can be in a larger one. Each respective business is on its own to attract capital by producing an adequate income stream and return on investment. Each of the businesses are insulated from the risks involved in the other business. Divesting also may free resources that were previously dedicated to the divested segment. These resources are then free to be invested into new undertakings or to reinforce existing operations. In addition to more obvious potential advantages, divestment might simplify a corporate portfolio of holdings that shareholders can better understand. As more and more divestitures appear in the business market, the American public, investors, employees, and government will accept divesting a business segment as an acceptable method of restructuring a corporation to better meet market competition.

Advantages to the divested segment often are overlooked. A number of constraints segment management had to deal with before may be lifted. Prohibitions against certain business activities may be removed. Restrictive labor practices may be improved. Management incentives may be renewed and managers themselves may find many bureaucratic requirements no longer are necessary. A rejuvenated organization within the former segment subsidiary may result.

A SOURCE OF CASH

A business segment may have a relatively small percentage of its assets in the form of cash. The other assets are generally a mix of near-cash and fixed assets. If the parent corporation is in serious need of cash, the sale of a business segment may produce the necessary cash to save the parent corporation from incurring more debt or filing for bankruptcy. Lending institutions are looking at sustaining cash flow in a downturn as a more important lending measure than ever before. This has enabled more corporations to borrow funds than was possible a decade ago.[2] In the case of a corporation already in a Chapter 11 reorganization, the sale of assets or entire segments may be necessary to return the parent corporation from the court directed bankruptcy arrangements. In a portion of its recent start at reorganization, Texaco Inc. chose to assign foreign-based refining assets to a joint venture and the outright sale of oil sources, producing, refining, and distribution assets. The cash proceeds will be used to satisfy the companies' long litigation with Pennzoil Co.[3]

A partial divestiture technique of offering an initial public offering for a minority of a subsidiary's stock, and then spinning off the remaining subsidiary stock shares to stockholders of the parent corporation provides two benefits. First, the minority shares of the subsidiary sold to the public generate cash, which can be used to improve operations or acquire new subsidiaries. Second, control of the subsidiary remains with the parent's shareholders. Subsidiary shares held by the parent's shareholders may increase in value if the subsidiary does well and a market has been established in the subsidiary stock. If the parent corporation retains 80 percent or more of the subsidiary stock, the parent can prepare consolidated financial statements and combine subsidiary income with the parent. This allows the parent to retain access to any tax credits the subsidiary maintains.

Although corporate restructuring, including large numbers of divestitures, has left the American companies leaner in their individual operations, it also has left them more heavily in debt. Stock buy backs, takeovers, takeover defenses, and sales of companies to their managements are pushing them ever further into debt. During the 1981–82 recession, annual corporate defaults climbed to more than $840 million from $60 million during a prior period. The American economy has had a long series of sound growth, but defaults also continue to grow. In 1987 defaults reached $9 billion. Acquisitions activity has increased. "Once the economy begins to weaken, as it sooner or later will, the high levels of corporate debt will exacerbate the downturn. A company in trouble can simply cut or suspend dividend payments on stock but will go bankrupt if it can't service its debt," stated M. D. Levy, chief economist of First Fidelity Bancorp in Philadelphia. Nonfinancial corporation debt was $1.8 trillion in 1987, three times the debt amount of $586.2 billion in 1976. The growth rate of debt from the mid-1970s has been faster than earnings growth.[4]

In early 1988 Texaco Inc. planned to sell its European refining assets as an integral part of its restructuring efforts. The $3 billion in proceeds would be used to help retire $5.5 billion Texaco owes creditors. This was designed to help Texaco emerge from Chapter 11 protection of the U.S. Bankruptcy Code.[5]

In June 1988 the USX Corporation announced that it would sell the majority share in its extensive barge and railroad lines to an investment bank, the Blackstone Group. USX has followed a lengthy strategy of selling assets to pay for its expensive diversification into the oil industry. The 1988 sale is the largest for the company since the 1986 public sale of its chemical operations for $570 million. The barge and freight lines carry coal and iron ore for USX and have a book value of approximately $500 million. The proceeds will be used to cut the corporation's $6.6 billion debt. The debt was incurred when USX purchased Marathon Oil Co. in 1982 for $5.93 billion in cash and notes and, in 1986, bought Texas Oil & Gas Corporation for $3 billion in stock. To pay for Marathon, it sold $5 billion in assets, including coal reserves, timberland, and the corporate headquarters. The 1988 asset sale reaffirms the corporate chairman's tendency to hold assets until they peak in market value and then sell them. In this case, the segment sales proceeds will be used to retire debt of earlier diversifications.[6]

In 1988 Tenneco asked $5 to $7 billion for its oil and gas properties. The chairman and CEO said, "The majority of the proceeds will go to debt restructuring." The very large amount of debt on its books, $6.4 billion, provided a debt-to-equity ratio above 65 percent. Tenneco collected most of this debt by expanding during two of the most severe downturns in their primary businesses, agriculture and energy. Since then, stockbrokers had suggested restructuring the corporation. It has been rumored as a takeover target because of its liquidation value, but using the proceeds to retire debt, it will reduce its debt-to-equity ratio and apply the cash to reduce its attraction to takeover.[7]

Of course, extra cash from a divestiture is not restricted to retiring debt. It can be used for general corporate purposes as CSX Corporation did when it sold its gas and oil unit in 1988. CSX is the parent corporation of a troubled railroad. Management used proceeds to offer voluntary severance payments to railroad workers in an effort to reach its corporate goal of cutting 12,000 employees, about 30 percent of its railroad work force. Enough of the proceeds will remain to retire some debt and maintain funds in dealing with rail labor.[8]

Divestiture cash can be used for further takeovers as Coastal Corporation also did in 1988. Management planned to sell a half interest in its six U.S. oil refineries which have a processing capacity of six percent of the total U.S. oil refining capacity.

In addition, its 233 refined product terminals and 850 Derby trade name gasoline stations would be included in the sale. Cash would be used to retire debt but the balance would be available for acquisitions which strongly interests the CEO.[9]

A use for divestiture cash that has become more common than in prior decades is to repurchase shares in ones own corporation in defense of a hostile takeover. In 1986 Union Carbide sold its consumer products businesses, its engineering polymers and composites business, its chromium, vanadium, and tungsten businesses, and buildings and 275 acres in Westchester County, New York. The entire amount, approximately $700 million, was used to buy back its own shares under a tender offer, increase the regular dividend on remaining shares and the preparation of a shareholder-rights plan to ensure each shareholder would receive $85 per share in any business combination. All of this divestiture activity was in response to a hostile takeover bid by GAF.[10]

As the tables in Chapter 1 indicate, some corporate divestitures are very large. Beatrice Companies has been an active acquirer and divester of corporations. According to W. T. Grimm & Co., Beatrice has sold 60 segment and subsidiaries since 1979; many were obtained earlier in large conglomerates acquisitions. Beatrice sold its E-II Holdings Inc., formerly called Esmark, to American Brands Inc. for $1.1 billion. From 1986 through 1987, Beatrice Companies sold or took public eight major segments including International Playtex Inc.'s personal products lines and the Avis rental car chain. The latter two subsidiaries were sold for a combined $6.1 billion. Beatrice has become known as a corporation selling most of its divestitures at what is considered top market dollar.[11]

Although not a true segment divestiture, Santa Fe Pacific Realty, a division of the combined Santa Fe Industries and Southern Pacific Co., sold 8 million square feet in developed and fully leased buildings in 1988 with a goal of selling all buildings by 1992. This asset sale is to raise cash to pay off loans and subordinated debentures issued for the merger.[12]

In an overt divestiture, General Mills placed two of their clothing chains up for sale. The cash proceeds from the sale of the Talbots and Eddie Bauer stores would help finance the parent's aggressive investment plans and provide monies to increase the company's stock buy-back program.[13] As with any marketable asset, the conversion of it to cash enables the owner to apply the newly gained liquid asset to other needs of the organization.

THE PLANNING PROCESS

An operation as complex as the divestiture of a business segment requires extensive planning, including a definition of the relationship between the parent and the subsidiary during the period before and after the divestiture. A corporation has strategic objectives, although many corporate managements don't recognize their existence. Corporations have chosen to be the biggest in their industry or geographic area; some have decided to become a conglomerate with business interests in different but related industries. Other companies chose to become active in any business where they can make an adequate profit. Corporations are in some businesses for reasons of history or for little or no apparent rational reason.

Gould Inc. focuses its corporate image on its defense systems, minicomputer technology, factory automation, test and measurement medical instrumentation, and custom-designed computer chips. During the 1970s and early 1980s, Gould sold all of its industrial businesses such as engine parts and ball bearings and used the money to acquire companies with leading positions in a particular segment of the electronics markets. Management became obsessed with being a high tech company and nothing but high tech. In 1983 Gould discovered a technique to build a lightweight engine battery with 40 percent more starting power than conventional batteries. Although it was introduced in a test market with no advertising, its sales exceeded twice the anticipated sales levels. In response, corporate management proposed selling the battery division because the battery business had a return on investment of only 10 percent compared with a 20 percent plus for the electronics divisions. Refocusing the corporation on high tech left batteries "clearly the square peg in this round hole."[14]

When the management consciously redirects the corporation

from one business area to another, this refocusing may include divesting segments that no longer fit the new structure or image management perceives for the corporation. For example, Chemical Bank put its $2.38 billion British home mortgage business up for sale so that it could free capital for a change of direction into more profitable businesses. Although the British mortgage business has been profitable, it doesn't meet the bank's long-term strategic objectives. On the United Kingdom side, the divestiture is a retrenchment. The bank needs the capital to support its banking operations globally. The strategic plan is to divest itself of marginally profitable operations outside the United States in order to concentrate on more profitable international trading and fund management businesses. The effort requires a redeployment of its assets. The refocusing has resulted from a rules change by the U.S. Federal Reserve Board, which requires U.S. banks to hold twice as much capital in reserve for non-U.S. mortgages than it does for domestic mortgages. This puts Chemical Bank at a competitive disadvantage.[15] A federal regulation change caused a strategic refocusing of a domestic bank's business strategy, which in turn caused the bank to divest a large segment of its business. Merrill Lynch announced in 1987 a retreat from the strategy of offering virtually every type of financial services by putting their real estate business up for sale. They used the proceeds to extend the core securities business on a global scale.[16]

One of the difficult divestiture factors management has to overcome is decision-making inertia. Santa Fe Southern Pacific in 1988 placed $300 million worth of real estate for sale after first thinking of putting it into a real estate investment trust. A company representative was quoted as saying, "The real estate investment trust had been the first shot at rethinking the real estate strategy."[17] Analyst Schwarzman of Lehman Brothers Kuhn Loeb said, "If you blow the timing on a restructuring, you blow the whole thing. You've got to sell cyclical assets at the top of their cycle or forget it." Consultant Mitchell of the consulting firm Mitchell & Co. added, "There are a lot of companies that came up with the brilliant insight last December that they had this business that they ought not to be involved with. Lo and behold, when they got themselves organized to do something about it, it was February and the wrong time to sell. It will be three years or more before they see the prices they missed."[18]

Some corporations have tried to change their consumer image by divestitures. Montgomery Ward's financial turnaround is at least partially due to the transformation from a general merchandiser to a "value-driven chain of specialty stores." Ward sold Jefferson Ward discount stores, discontinued its catalog business and dropped marginal lines of merchandise. The restructuring including grouping goods into specialty shops within each Wards store. Management even began to lease vacant store space to Toys R Us to build pedestrian customer traffic. In 1987 Ward opened free-standing specialty shops focused on appliances, home furnishings, auto parts, and jewelry.[19] Divestiture was a major part of their restructuring after management had shifted the business focus from one type of merchandising to another.

As mentioned earlier, General Mills has gone through a major restructuring and redirection in its business lines. Besides the sale of the Talbots and Eddie Bauer clothing chains, corporate management has decided to concentrate on its food operations by continuing to divest its nonfood businesses. In 1985 management began the specific divestiture plan by spinning off its toy business to create Kenner Parker Toys Inc., its fashion lines as Izod and Ship'N Shore stores, and the Monet jewelry unit into Crystal Brands Inc. Between 1985 and 1988, General Mills management had sold its crafts business, a wallpaper retailer, and a chain of sportswear stores. However, in 1987 the board of directors softened the food business focus by authorizing 20 new outlets and the introduction of a children's line in the Eddie Bauer stores. In addition, the board was prepared to spend $190 million for expanding the Talbot stores into direct marketing and store renewal. In early 1988 management pointed out to the board that costs of competing for catalog customers during the recently passed Christmas season were very high and the company's specialty retailing earnings had dropped 13 percent in the last quarter of 1987. During the first quarter of 1988, the board returned to the original refocusing plan toward becoming an all food products corporation.[20] Apparently divestiture will continue at General Mills as an integral part of their corporate refocusing.

Have other corporations used general planning guidelines to determine when a business should be divested? Crown Cork & Seal Co. has emphasized profits rather than sales levels. Even though a reduction in the total corporate sales levels would result, Crown management decided to divest the oil can business because it had more profitable opportunities available. This decision was made when the company had 50 percent of the oil can market. Fiberfoil oil cans were posing too great a threat to Crown's older design can so rather than revamp their production operations, Crown sold the business.[21] In another example, Olin sold its Ecusta cigarette paper business because it didn't meet Olin's performance standards.[22]

A problem many corporations face when divestiture planning is mentioned is "Who will do it?" In most operational companies, divestiture experience is nonexistent. Vignola found that the divestment was diffused throughout the company. Over half of his respondents thought that divestiture had a definite place in the planning process. The diffusion of which department assigned someone to investigate the divestiture situation within corporations and the percentage of responding companies are shown below.[23]

Department	Percent of Responding Companies
Planning group	54%
Division management	29%
President's office	25%
Finance department	25%

Such diversity makes standardizations difficult.

DIVESTITURE AS A POSITIVE SOLUTION SUMMATION

Divestiture may be the best alternative available for the corporation. Divestiture should be thought of as a positive corporate solution to a difficult management problem. Divestiture is a source of cash to meet the various needs a corporation may require above the periodic operational cash flow. The planning process for a divestiture is very important for a successful separation.

11

Divestiture Segment Valuation

One of the early considerations in divestiture determination is developing a value of the business segment that is subject to divestiture. Valuation has both an objective and a subjective component. Considerations in valuing a segment for divestiture include the:

1. Valuation range
2. Financial statements
3. Potential buyers
4. Fairness opinions

VALUATION RANGE

The first step is to maximize the value realized by the buyer and to establish the maximum defensible value range for the business unit. The minimum value would be the liquidation value of the net assets. The maximum value in the range should reflect the net present value of expected returns of the business segment based on cash flow projections, discounted at a rate of return reflecting optimism, and confidence in the future of the divested segment. Segment cash flow is defined as:

Segment Cash Flow = Business Segment Operating Profit × (1 − Corporate Income Tax Rate) + Segment

Depreciation + Other Noncash Income Statement Items — Additional Segment Working Capital Required — Additional Segment Fixed Capital Required

The stream of cash flows, which may vary from year to year, should be discounted to the present time. The discount factor used should be based on the cost of capital at the minimum acceptable rate of return on new investments. This rate should reflect the risk inherent in purchasing the divested business segment. One estimate of the discount factor can be based on what interest rate an investor would require if he were to invest in a corporate security with the same inherent risk as the divested segment. A columnar presentation of the yearly cash flows can be discounted to the present using a table of discount factors, or a calculator or computer programmed for such calculations. The result is the net present value of the projected cash flows at the interest rate required for such an investment.

It depends on the market dealings between buyer and seller as to what value is assigned to the divestiture. Within the Japanese business buying community, in general, they take a slow, methodical approach to acquiring a company. Valuation is done very carefully with strategic considerations as the principal objective. European investors use more of a "full speed ahead" approach, often using quickness and surprise in their bids. Negotiating a divestiture with either of these two groups of potential buyers requires greatly differing levels of patience.[1]

A proposed divestiture sale price may be at the top of the range of values. In 1989 the Loral Corporation agreed to sell its two nondefense electronics divisions to a group led by the company's chairman and chief executive officer for $400 million in cash and a debenture that Loral values at $25 million. An investment bank advising Loral on the sale, Lazard Freres & Co., had determined a range of potential values Loral could expect. Some aerospace analysts also said that the proposed sale price is much higher than they expected Loral to get for the businesses. One analyst for Drexel Burnham Lambert Inc. of New York was quoted as saying that the two divisions were widely known to bring less than the $400 million offered. No explanation was given for the large offer.[2]

FINANCIAL STATEMENTS

A set of pro forma financial statements for the divested segment should be prepared for the potential purchasers. Included with the statements should be the various assumptions inherent in the statements. A sensitivity analysis of financial performance, including the associated net present values, to changes in the pro forma assumptions should be prepared to determine their impact and to isolate those changes that are significant.

A substantial exit barrier can develop when the firm becomes reluctant to sell or abandon its investments in a particular business because it cannot retrieve their value. The entry barriers that firms overcome in competing become the very forces that will deter their departure later. Competition within some declining industries may be marred by panicky behavior resulting in substantial writeoffs of assets and destructive rounds of price-cutting as firms burdened with excessive productive capacity try to fill these plants to break even levels. The value of these assets would soften over time as the recognition of industry-wide decline became increasingly widespread.[3]

POTENTIAL BUYERS

The next step is to identify the optimal group of potential buyers. It becomes the job of the divesting company to consummate a deal with one of the potential buyers at a price as close as possible to the maximum end of the defensible value range while the potential buyer is striving for the lowest range value. Hopefully to the seller, the price will exceed the liquidation or breakup value of the segment.

FAIRNESS OPINIONS

Fairness opinions from third parties are used to determine the value of divestitures as well as the many other types of transfers of value. Often investment banks are chosen to provide these opinions. A fairness opinion, which is addressed to a board of directors, expresses the investment banker's opinion that the price paid in the transaction is "fair from a financial point of view" to the shareholders of the company. The importance of the opinion varies depending on the context in which it is rendered. The investment banks may deliver the opinions management wants because of the large fee involved. The securities laws require management to treat all stockholders fairly but fairness is a subjective item. In mergers, investment bankers usually define fairness by considering liquidation value, the current value of a company's future cash flow and its financial ranking against others in the same industry. The same bases can be used in evaluating the value of a divestiture. If stockholders think valuations are set unfairly, a New York appeals court ruled in April 1988 that shareholders could sue investment banks over fairness opinions. The size of an investment bank's fee is frequently dependent on the outcome of a takeover, buyout, or divestiture and the fairness opinion clearly can influence that outcome.[4]

Also participating in occasional fairness opinions, commercial banks have begun to function as investment banks. This has raised the question of potential disloyalty to their corporate clients because of the banks' intimate knowledge of the corporation's finances during acquisition-divestiture negotiations.

VALUATION SUMMATION

Valuation of the business segment as an independent entity or as part of another corporation is always going to be a subjective and difficult figure to estimate. The minimum generally is the liquidation value and the maximum is the net present value of an optimistic sales and profit projection. Somewhere within this range is the fair value. Although these valuation methods are used, it should be remembered that the sum of the corporation's parts may be greater in value than the whole corporation. In addition, the components of a corporation may be sold more easily than the whole complex corporation itself. Therefore, divestiture is a technique that may be the best alternative available as a corporation changes its focus in a changing economic environment.

Divestiture negotiations should include a set of pro forma

financial statements of the business segment to be divested. These should be presented to the potential buyers. Third parties may be asked to provide a fairness opinion on the valuation of the segment.

12

Effects on Resources

Divestiture has serious and significant impacts on corporate resources. Management should consider the changes in the areas of:

1. Product and activity mix
2. Reallocation of strategic resources
3. Corporate financial implications, including stock market reactions, debt rating reactions, and tax considerations

When management begins a corporate restructuring, they need to consider how the proposed changes will affect the product mix.

PRODUCT AND ACTIVITY MIX

Will the divestiture disrupt other corporate production or distribution operations? Are the facilities of the divested segment shared or used by any other corporate activity? Are there any downstream products or processes dependent on the divested operation? Does the corporation now produce a raw material or intermediate product upstream that may not have a market because the divested business will belong to new owners? Will marketing be seriously impacted because the divested products or services will no longer be available to sell? Will the corporation be introducing a new market competitor or significantly helping a present competitor? Is this divestiture really worth all this trouble? That's the feeling of many managers when they confront all the divestiture details of an ongoing operation. Some have been critical of the recent American tendency to create only financial corporate restructuring rather than operational improvement changes. For example, Eugene Lerner, a finance professor at Northwestern University, was outspoken on the analysis American business put into restructuring. He said, "Every one of them wants to be dealt a new hand. They screwed up once and now they want to try again. I don't think they should be allowed to. As long as they are going to play portfolio games and the Japanese are going to play with real things, this country is going to get whipped."[1]

REALLOCATION OF STRATEGIC RESOURCES

One of the principal reasons for divestiture is to allow corporate management to reallocate resources from the divested entity to other operations that have a higher possibility of growth or profitability, or that fit the strategic corporate direction better than the divested segment. If the divested business had been troubled, management efforts would have been concentrated on it at the expense of the rest of the corporation. After the merger of National and Pan Am Airlines, the merging of work forces and international competition combined to distract corporate management to the point that they neglected to reshuffle the domestic air routes which was the primary purpose of the merger. Profits have suffered since the merger.[2] Michael Seely, president of investor Access Corporation contends, "In the past decade only one-third of all mergers have enriched the acquirer's shareholders, one-third have been a wash, and one-third have ended up costing investors money."[3] Textron, after many successful acquisitions, decided to restructure in 1985 because, "It doesn't want to be a conglomerate anymore. It wants to concentrate on defense and financial services, two fields that are currently thought to be hot. To raise money and change its image, it wants to get rid of businesses that don't fit, even if they are profitable."[4]

George Sella, Jr., chairman of American Cyanamid Co., planned to turn the 80-year old company into a smart, modern entrepreneurial outfit by selling, along with other restructuring moves, the consumer products division. The division was a collection of brand names that Cyanamid never had the marketing ability to capitalize. He believed you build a company by selling the laggard parts for the benefit of the good parts.[5]

According to Ralph Hellmold, Shearson Lehman Brothers, when a business is divested from a corporation, "the real issue then becomes whether you can redeploy all of that capital in your basic business. If you can't grow the crown jewel any faster than you're growing it anyway, you have a much more interesting intellectual argument, but probably one that management isn't interested in."[6]

A fixed asset intensive division with aging equipment requires inflows of cash to update, replace and upgrade the fixed assets if it is going to successfully compete in the global markets. If the results after improving the assets are not particularly financially attractive, the corporation appears to be "pouring good money after bad." Divestiture becomes a viable alternative.

Without a strong sense of where the corporation wants to go and what businesses it is in, management will most probably allocate financial and management resources in an ad hoc manner. Profit maximization would not be feasible. With divestiture, operational simplicity may be frittered away. If the stock market sees that the corporation invests the proceeds in an equally disparate activity where the management has no competence, the corporate stock price invariably goes down. Management has to use the divestiture to move resources to demonstrated areas of high corporate potential. Higher than the business divested, if the divestiture is to be considered successful.

CORPORATE FINANCIAL IMPLICATIONS

The cost of capital is a significant factor in most corporate income statements. Diversified corporations have a problem not faced by the one business company. As companies become more diversified and the nature of their business becomes less clearly defined, investor uncertainty with respect to a company's risks and opportunities will increase. The greater the uncertainty, the higher the risk premium demanded by the equity investor and lender. A higher cost of capital, both equity and liabilities, results.[7]

There are a growing number of corporations coming under intense pressure from stockholders to achieve the best possible value for their stock.

Stock Market Reactions

When a segment is divested, the stock market is going to revalue the market valuation of both the parent and the divested segment. If the segment was a financial drain on the parent, divestiture can be favorably valued by the market. If the parent divests the valuable assets of the corporation, as viewed by the stock market, the traded common stock of the parent may drop, sometimes steeply. *Forbes* magazine published a table of such comparisons in 1985 and *Dun's Business Month* did likewise in 1986. A selected set of changes in the parent's common stock price from the *Forbes'* 1985 and the 1986 *Dun's Business Month* articles are combined and shown in Table 12.1. As perceived by the stock market, not all parent corporations shed "losers." All other market or economic factors are not *excluded* from the prior share price change table, so the table data must be considered as interesting but not conclusive.

Under a plan to boost stockholder values, Amfac Inc. sold its distribution, food, and mainland resort operations, which represented 75 percent of Amfac's 1987 revenue. However, because of problems at one of the units, they provided a much smaller portion of operating profit. Net proceeds were returned to the stockholders. Management also planned to sell up to 50 percent of its substantial Hawaii land holdings and return these proceeds to stockholders. After the dispositions, the company will focus on its Hawaiian retailing and landholding operations. The stock market favorably viewed the announcement.[8]

The stock market as well as the stockholder closely follows corporate earnings per share (EPS). A divested segment may have been capital intensive, unprofitable, or had poor returns

Table 12.1
**Changes in Common Stock Prices Before and After Major
Divestitures**

Parent	Divestiture date	Approximate percentage change from divestiture date to 1985 or 1986
Amer Natural Res	1982	+95% (1985)
General Mills	1984	+79% (1986)
Mesa Petroleum	1982	+59% (1985)
RJ Reynolds Inds	1984	+44% (1985)
AT&T	1984	+24% (1985)
Time Inc.	1984	− 7% (1985)
Centex	1984	− 8% (1985)
Singer Co.	1986	− 9% (1986)
Allied Signal	1985	−13% (1986)
Texas Intern	1982	−81% (1985)

Source: L. Pittel, "The Parts and the Whole," *Forbes*, March 25, 1985, pp. 264–268; J. Perham, "Business Kicks Out the Turkeys," *Dun's Business Month*, September 1986, pp. 30–34.

on investment. A June 1985 *Forbes* magazine article listed more than 10 corporations that had sold segments during the prior three years (1982–85) with positive effects on the parent corporation's EPS. Several of the corporations are included in Table 12.2. Over the same time period, sales had decreased from 44 to 7 percent for these specific corporations. Divestiture was very favorable to the earnings per share for a number of U.S. corporations.

In the case of General Nutrition Inc., the company's common stock increased from $2.625 per share in 1987 to $9.00 per share in the first quarter of 1989. Company management attributed the increase to its recent corporate restructuring including shedding its mail-order business, consolidating manufacturing operations, and closing more than 300 unprofitable stores. The company was ready to plan for future growth. Alternatives for the cash flow-rich corporation included a sale of the company, a recapitalization, an expanded stock buy-back program, and a

Table 12.2
Changes in Parent Corporation's EPS After Divestitures

Corporation/Business	Percentage Change in EPS, 1982–85	Units Sold
Banner Inds/industrial machinery	+318%	Trucking Business
Occidental Petro/oil & gas producers	+346%	Domestic crude & trans.
Gulf & Western Inds/multicompany	+ 65%	46 widely diff.
Howell Corp./oil & gas producers	+ 47%	Gas pipe, oil, gas prop.
Exxon/oil & gas prod.	+ 40%	Refin., serv., office sys.
Ingersoll-Rand/indus. mach.	+ 15%	Hand & cut. tools
Universal Leaf Tobacco/tobacco	+ 13%	Fert. plts.
Chevron/oil & gas prod.	+ 11%	Eur. refin.

Source: L. Pittel, "Smaller Can Be Prettier," *Forbes*, June 17, 1985, pp. 206–208.

leveraged buyout. Divestiture and the related restructuring of its business operations turned the company into a debt free and profitable organization.[9]

Debt-Rating Reactions

In the winter 1985 issue of *Mergers & Acquisitions*, Gail Hessol stated that "Mergers, acquisitions and divestitures represented the largest single cause of changes in Standard & Poor's debt ratings of industrial companies during 1984."[10] The same can be said for the current time. Mergers, acquisitions, and divestitures are major changes in the corporation structure and the way it operates. When a divested property gains independence, there is a need to inaugurate ratings of the new company on a stand-alone basis. The anaylsis is focused on what has changed. Particular attention is paid to the near-term earnings stability of both the parent and the new stand-alone divestiture. The debt market also reflects this significant change. The divested segment may assume debt once carried by the parent corporation, or the segment may *not* be assigned any debt upon divestiture. Either situation will effect the debt ratios, the ability to retire the debt, and the resulting Standard & Poor's debt ratings.

Beatrice Company had to review its debt situation because it found the $1.1 billion in miscellaneous liabilities were becoming a troublesome factor in divestiture negotiations. First Boston, an investment banker, studied ways to parcel the liabilities to the segments sold. The alternative not favored by Beatrice management was for the parent corporation to absorb the entire $1.1 billion debt.[11]

The Tyler Corporation management planned to sell their Reliance Universal unit for $275 million. Half of this sale price was the assumption of Tyler debt at $189 million. Reliance is an industrial coatings maker based in Louisville, Kentucky, and the Tyler Corporation is a holding company. Last year Tyler sold its Hall-Mark Electronics unit for $200 million in cash and $30 million in notes.[12]

As another example, four 1984–85 divestitures affected the debt ratings of the parent corporation as shown in Table 12.3. The table figures indicate that the results of the divestiture can be far reaching, well beyond daily operations. If either the parent or the now freestanding segment plans to return to the debt market in the near future, the amount of debt, particularly from debt assumption or leveraged buy-outs, has to be taken into consideration in both payment of principal and interest, and its effect on the debt ratings for future borrowing.

Although every businessperson understands that debt can force unplanned business decisions at inappropriate times, Newmont Mining Corporation, which had to borrow $2.1 billion to pay a special dividend to fend off a corporate takeover by T. Boone Pickens, Jr., had hoped to pay off much of the debt by selling only nongold assets. However, the stock market

Table 12.3
Divesting Corporations

Divesting Corporation	Divested Operation	Standard & Poor's Rating of the Parent Senior Debt/ Commercial Paper	
		Before	After
Beatrice Company	Chem Operations	AA/A-1	A/A-2
RCA Corporation	CIT Fin/Hertz	BBB+/ A-2	A-/A- 2
Texaco Inc.	Employers Reinsur	AA+/ A- 1+	AA-/ A- 1+

Source: G. Hessol, "Debt Rating Revisions: Aftermath of Mergers," *Mergers & Acquisitions*, Winter 1985, pp. 42–47.

"crash" of 1987 reduced the assets' market value to such a level that their sale would not retire significant portions of the debt. By selling their holdings in Du Pont and much of their interest in Foote Mineral, management reduced the debt from $2.1 billion to $1.6 billion. Because of the high level of remaining debt, Newmont Mining was forced into divestiture of their Australian gold mining subsidiary, Newmont Australia.[13]

Parent companies rarely make statements of nonguarantee of subsidiary debt, preferring to leave their intentions ambiguous. This allows them maximum flexibility, and if a lender to a subsidiary desires a guarantee from the parent, it is generally expected to be in writing and explicit.[14]

Tax Considerations

Tax considerations are often a significant factor in divestitures. With tax law and its interpretations changing nearly monthly, the tax implications of a divestiture have to be determined when a divestiture is implemented. For example, General Electric and Dun & Bradstreet corporations began selling their television stations in 1983. Tax breaks were considered to be the deciding factor in the divestitures. As an intentional or unintentional encouragement, the tax consequences favored divesting the stations. Sellers could receive cash for the sale at a then capital gains tax rate on the stations' earnings and market value. Without selling, GE and D & B had exhausted much of their tax benefits because all of the depreciation had been claimed. Any rising stream of earnings would be taxed on its full amount. However, buyers could begin the depreciation based on the purchase price, not the original historical cost. Depreciation deductions were elevated because the exchange value had risen from when the station was first purchased by GE or D & B. In addition, GE's broadcast group is only 39th in size in the nation, and GE management decided to be first or second in all markets it serves.[15]

RESOURCE EFFECTS SUMMATION

Divestiture effects on corporate resources must be considered when divestiture planning is conducted. Effects on the product and activity mix of the corporation and the interrelations of manufacturing and distribution have to be considered. Financial considerations due to the divestiture are the changes in the earnings per share, stock market reactions, tax considerations of divestiture, and changes in the corporate debt ratings. All of these factors need to be reviewed before a divestiture is implemented.

13

Managerial Implications of Divestiture

When divestiture is seriously considered as a strategic alternative, management of the divesting parent corporation has to take into considertaion the employees of the divested entity as well as the financial and physical implications. Long-time profit contributors, the first company product, or products closely associated with the corporation name are often areas of corporate pride and therefore take on special meaning to both management and employees.

Managerial participation in a divestiture must be concerned with:

1. Corporate culture
2. Employee morale
3. Management morale
4. Public relations
5. Operational implications

People working together toward a common goal form formal and informal organizations including communications, allegiances, and dependencies. All corporations have such commonalities that are often gathered under the term "the corporate culture."

CORPORATE CULTURE

W. B. Tunstall defined the corporate culture as "an amalgam of shared values, behavior patterns, mores, symbols, attitudes, and normative ways of conducting business that, more than its products or services, differentiate it from all other companies. Cultural uniqueness is a primary and cherished feature of organizations, a critical asset that is nurtured in the internal value system."[1] The corporate culture provides the togetherness and drive to move the corporation toward its strategic and tactical goals. The culture can be the difference between a successful and an also-ran corporation.

In extremely large corporations, the cultural climate plays a very important role in long-term performance. Bell Telephone's culture blended mutually reinforcing features such as lifetime careers, up-from-the-ranks management succession, dedication to customer service, operational skills, consensus management, level consciousness, and a strong focus on regulatory matters.[2] A regulated environment such as Bell's, with its culture of a slow steady progression for the majority of its employees and its bias toward deliberation, was suddenly told to change to a risk-oriented, marketplace mindset, individual performance organization with large differences in individual salaries, and a bias toward action. When Bell was ordered to divest its operating companies, it was a traumatic experience for a corporate culture that was built on a long self-supporting relationship. Bell management initiated efforts to redefine the corporate missions and reshape the corporate culture. Rumors travel rapidly through a company and even an industry when a major business activity is anticipated. A major divestiture such as the Bell Telephone breakup sent shock waves throughout the industry. Psychological damage may taint the image of both the segments and the parent. Misunderstandings and insecurities that arise during an extended sales or divestiture process may lead to the guilty portrayal of a thoughtless parent company with little sense of responsibility toward its employees, its community, and even its shareholders.

EMPLOYEE MORALE

There are many different ways to counter these occurrences. Rubin suggests that preserving strict confidentiality about the divestiture and restricting the size of the divestiture staff to a minimum is mandatory.[3] Vignola adds that the information from the two companies (assuming there are both buying and selling corporations rather than a Bell Telephone court-ordered divestiture) be consistent, especially as it relates to the jobs of the employees. The first priority is to stress the viability of the divested activity in the hands of the new owners.[4]

Senior management often concentrates on the technical aspects of divestiture, but overlooks the equally key area, managing the human side of organizational change. Most managers recognize that the corporation's human systems are far more complex than any financial or legal system. The complexity of the human component of a corporation may explain why senior executives concentrate on managing the financial aspects of a divestiture rather than the human and organizational portion. It is simply too complex and too resistant to certain solutions. Some divestiture failures can be traced to the lack of attention of the human and organizational changes involved.[5] Refer to the Kanter and Seggerman study discussed in Chapter 9 for the detrimental effects senior executives can have on the success of acquisitions.

Working with the employee union, if it exists, to clarify the situation is a better approach than developing an antagonistic attitude. Rail unions went to court under the Railway Labor Act and blocked the sale of the financially troubled Pittsburgh & Lake Erie Railroad. A court decision, upheld on appeal, required the P&LE to bargain with its unions over plans to cut the line's work force of 700 by 70 percent. This ruling "put a big wet sponge" over proposed short rail line sales.[6] Employees have read and heard of divestitures that have resulted in serious unemployment. At Olin in 1985 sales and shutdowns of several subsidiary businesses resulted in a work force reduction of 3,500 employees. In addition, another 700 salaried positions were eliminated as a continuation of the operating reduction program begun in 1983. The 4,200 employees affected amount to 25 percent of Olin's 17,000 member work force.[7] John Welch, Jr., chief executive officer of General Electric, remade the company from a smokestack giant to a high-tech behemoth. In the process, he sold over 200 businesses and spent $11 billion to purchase 300 new ones, closed 73 plants and facilities, and eliminated 131,000 jobs through divestiture, attrition, dismissal, and contract buyouts. According to Welch, no one is assured a lifetime job at General Electric, and no job would ever be finished. "Hire, train, motivate and compensate the best people and insist they search for problems. 'Don't fix it if it ain't broke' is a dangerous and silly adage," adds Lawrence Bossidy, a vice chairman of GE.[8] Employee morale could be a serious factor at a plant acquired or subject to divestiture at General Electric.

Kanter and Seggerman suggest six points that can aid management in guiding the human dimensions of business divestitures. The are:

1. Recognize that anxiety is inevitable in any major organizational change. Recognize the emotional issues and the impact the divestiture will have on the lives of the employees.

2. Strengthen vertical communication channels. Companies have used frequent employee meetings, special newsletters, and frequent departmental meetings to keep all the employees informed as the divestiture considerations advance. Carefully develop ways to ensure that top management hears the concerns of the employees and can be seen to act on them.

3. Be perceived as fair. The way the company handles layoffs or cutbacks will have long-lasting effects on the remaining employees. If the employees believe the process was conducted unfairly, their future commitment to the company is likely to be far lower than if they think the corporation treats all fairly.

4. Give employees some feeling of control. Increasing the employee's participation in the decision making is a method used by many corporations to increase their level of involvement and ownership in the divestiture process.

5. Use new structures to manage change. Temporary management structures can be more flexible and more responsive than conventional management structures that were designed for corporate continuity and stability.

6. Capitalize on the changes being made. Move in directions that are advantageous for the corporation.

7. Work with local companies and public agenices to place employees released because of the divestiture.

8. If financially feasible, provide early retirement to the employees affected by the divestiture.

9. Give notice of divestiture as early as possible to the employees while recognizing the need to keep negotiations confidential.

This may be the proper time to make other changes necessary to improve the corporation's change for success even if they are not associated with the divestiture.[9]

MANAGEMENT MORALE

D. Nees studied 14 divestitures and found that improved line management cooperation was gained by their participation in the divestment process. This led to successful divestiture experiences for the corporation involved. The initiation of divestment is a corporate management task, but the success of the actual divestiture involves lower line management.[10] Close communications during the divestiture process provide management with the opportunity to keep all employees informed of the new activities' direction. A "fire sale" atmosphere wreaks havoc in terms of employee and management morale.

It is even more important to keep the senior executives of the divested segment informed and ensure, as much as possible, their job security. Another company purchases a business segment for its assets, which includes its most valuable asset, its people. If senior management of the divested segment leaves before the divestiture or shortly afterward, the segment buyer may renegotiate the amount paid for the segment. In the case of a divested segment being on its own, the divestiture may be unsuccessful because the unit may fail. The loss of jobs and the general bad publicity associated with this particular divestiture technique will provide little positive public relations for the parent corporation.

Top-producing employees should be retained in the divested

entity. When Sears, Roebuck & Co. agreed to sell its Coldwell Banker commercial real estate unit to an employee and investor team, continued success depended on the retention of key employees. The chairman thought there would be no wholesale defections. To make sure the restructuring was financially attractive to the employees, the corporation made 50 percent of the company available to them. The other 50 percent will be held by the investor group composed of Westinghouse Electric Corporation, Bankers Trust New York, The Pittsburgh Mellon family, and the Carlyle Group. To induce top-producing sales personnel to stay with Coldwell Banker, Sears distributed 5 percent of the purchase price to approximately 600 top employees who stay with the new company one year. The investor group contributed additional stock to managers who stayed two years.

In spite of these incentives, defections did occur. A Los Angeles-based real estate firm hired four of Coldwell's top 20 brokers. An executive outside the Sears organization commented that Coldwell lost the wrong people and pointed to the Los Angeles situation as indicative of problems within Coldwell Banker.[11]

Besides employees and the public concerns, key management personnel of the divested entity may leave before the divestiture is complete. This can cancel the divestiture. Tenneco Inc. constructed financial incentives to keep "critical employees" working for the segment earmarked for divestiture, at least until the transaction was complete. The incentive packages varied from employee category to category depending on the corporation's definition of "critical." Some engineers and geologists were given 14 weeks salary, some accountants were given six weeks pay, and some oil and gas workers were offered an "income and benefits protection program" in case their jobs were eliminated after the sale was completed. All were given one year's worth of medical and dental benefits and a week-and-a-half's pay for every year worked at Tenneco. This was in recognition of the value key employees have in making a business segment attractive in a divestiture.[12]

Although divestiture negotiations are best done in private,

the results need to be communicated fully, accurately, and in a proper time to both employees and management.

PUBLIC RELATIONS

Public relations and how the corporation is perceived by the general public are important to any corporation. The divesting company has a particular interest in clarifying its public image. The immediate public is where the divested facilities are located. Will the employees keep their jobs? Will civic contributions and activities be continued? Will the facilities continue to be operated at all? The regional and national image is important for the corporation, both for assuring investors and customers. Suppliers have to be assured that it will be business as usual with the divested segment, at least until the divestiture can be settled.

In some cases, divestitures have helped clarify the public image of a corporation. Some corporations have not appeared committed to a particular industry because of a subsidiary operating in another competing industry. The divestiture of the "offending" subsidiary allayed fears of customers and suppliers that the corporation might not be committed to the primary industry because of its corporate interest in the "offending" subsidiary industry. Other similar divestitures motivated by marketing factors are those designed to separate potentially incompatible products or lines.[13]

The corporate identity exemplifies the aspirations and objectives and provides a rallying point for defining the corporation. As corporations divest segments, their identities are affected and inevitably altered. Names are the visible manifestations of corporate identity. During 1984, 871 American companies changed their corporate names with 60 percent triggered by either a merger, an acquisition or a divestiture. However, corporate identity involves more than changing and communicating a new name. The identity needs to project what makes the corporation special. It includes advertising, appearance of employees and facilities, logos, charitable giving, and quality of both product and service. Management can utilize a change in identity to signal a major redirection of its organization and purpose including an improved market position and operating performance.

The failure of good public relations can lead to serious consequences. The Newell Co. closed its Clarksburg, West Virginia, glassmaking plant in 1988 and decided to move the glassmaking equipment to another of their facilities. However, a state legislator was ready to blockade the factory doors with a bulldozer to keep the company from removing the equipment. Governor A. A. Moore, Jr., filed a $614.6 million lawsuit against the Newell Co. charging a breach-of-contract. The governor says that states and communities are tired of throwing money and favors at companies to win or preserve jobs; the people now want what is due them. People are using public outrage, political pressure, and legal leverage to extract compensation well above what any existing union contracts and employee picket lines have yielded. Newell has paid $1 million to date to aid workers, and is discussing other repatriations with the state, including the possibility of reopening the plant. Meanwhile, the plant equipment remains locked up in Clarksburg.[14]

Harley Shaiken, labor professor at the University of California, San Diego, says, "Companies used to seek incentives to move into an area. Now, they're paying incentives to move out." The *Wall Street Journal* calls it a backlash to the deluge of factory shutdowns and heavy layoffs flowing from the feverish takeovers, near-takeovers, mergers, buyouts and divestitures of recent years.[15] Poor public relations can defeat the best planned divestiture.

OPERATIONAL IMPLICATIONS

Operational considerations are generally more obvious than personnel and financial complications. Integrated operations have to be carefully analyzed before the production/distribution stream can be broken by a divestiture. Customers, suppliers, and those with other types of working relationships with the corporation may be put into jeopardy by the contemplated divestiture. Breaking the production chain may require transitional sources of supply for intermediate materials for the divesting company's remaining products and services. Subtle difficulties may arise to areas such as with the corporate information systems. Will the divestiture cause serious problems in providing the necessary operational information for the remaining segments? Will the lower sales volume result in uneconomic production runs of the company's other products? How are the marketing and distribution systems dependent on the sales volume of the divested operations? Does an analysis of these considerations make the divestiture decision seem unwise?

MANAGERIAL IMPLICATIONS SUMMATION

Divestitures introduce corporate changes in managerial categories other than financial. The corporate culture, management and employee morale, public relations, and operational considerations must be taken into consideration when a divestiture is planned and implemented. The parent corporation's management must be very aware of the detrimental effects of any of these areas on the long-term positive results of a divestiture.

14

Divestiture and Stress

Divestitures can be very stressful events for the individuals involved with the business. Management, employees, stockholders, suppliers, and creditors will be under different amounts of stress during and after a divestiture. Differing aspects of looking at stress are:

1. The Social Readjustment Rating Scale
2. Stressor stimuli
3. External mediating factors
4. Internal mediating factors

Significant changes in the life-style of an individual often raise such questions as "What effect will it have on me?" or "How will I cope with it?" Former patterns of behavior and reactions that once brought satisfaction and reward may now bring only displeasure and even pain. Unless an adjustment is made, the person can become frustrated and even demoralized. In the work environment, workers can be called on to accept changes that are hard to make. If they receive little help from management in making the adjustments, it may take a long time, even years, for complete adjustment to the new business environment. During the period of adjustment, the business can be thought of as in a state of disequilibrium or unbalance.[1]

In divestiture situations, middle managers in the divested segment may feel the reason the parent corporation is divesting the unit is caused by their failure on the job. The psychological effects may be far-reaching. In the case of the 1930s Great Depression, many men are reported to have never recovered personally from its effects. If the manager or employee has been living with a large home mortgage, car loans and credit card balances, a divestiture of their work unit can be personally depressing.

At the supervisory and executive levels, the organizational changes may be perceived as affecting their status relationships with their professional peers in other corporations or the parent corporation. Serious reactions and anxieties can result. Corporate life can be viewed as a series of small and simple events. A disruption of these events, or their timing, change an individual's work life and can lead to irritation or "irrational" behavior. Adjusting to the changes may require a number of minor adjustments some employees are not willing to make. Their life isn't the same and they resent the changes.

The resentment can present itself in different ways. Physical effects such as coronary heart disease, peptic ulcers, and general deterioration of a person's general physical health can result. Employees also can experience psychological consequences including a general dissatisfaction with one's life, low self-esteem, psychological fatigue, boredom, resentment directed toward the job, and depression. Behavioral consequences including increased smoking or a reduced ability to quit smoking, increased drinking, and marital discord can result from changes in the job environment.

Employees under too much job stress tend to be frequently absent from work, become less involved with their work, and are more likely to quit their jobs. Some employees may quit caring about their work. These reactions are attempts to cope with the excessive stress. If the stress continues over a long period of time, all of the conditions and reactions are aggravated.[2]

If the manager reduces the adverse stress by harming the ability of the organization to compete in the marketplace, most managers will consider the welfare of the organization over that of the employee. However, most techniques used in divestiture situations to reduce stress do not reduce the effectiveness of the corporation. Reducing the excessive stress and uncertainty of the situation will: (1) Make employees stronger and more capable of good job performance; (2) reduce absenteeism due to illness; and (3) result in employees with higher self-esteem and the desire to perform well in order to keep self-esteem high.[3]

THE SOCIAL READJUSTMENT RATING SCALE

One term that psychologists use to describe life events is social readjustments. R. H. Rahe assigned weights to each social readjustment event and labelled it the Social Readjustment Rating Scale (SRRS). The scale is composed of 43 life events ranging from the death of a spouse to minor violations of the law. Each event was given a numerical weight to indicate its intensity and the length of time necessary for its accommodation. The scale ratings were obtained by asking 394 subjects to complete a written questionnaire rating the life events by the readjustment required. Marriage was assigned an arbitrary value of 50. Subjects were then asked if each other life event required a longer or shorter readjustment, compared to marriage, and to assign a proportionately larger or smaller value.

The numerical weights given to all events happening within a specific period of time were added together and the total was described as the Life Change Units (LCU) accumulated during that time. The LCUs were compared to the appearance of illness or the application for medical treatment in the same or subsequent time periods. Other researchers have used the SRRS concept in their analysis of stress and stress reactions in humans.

Several life events can be associated with major business changes such as being involved as a manager or employee in a divestiture. The specific life events described by Rahe dealing with divestiture trauma are shown in Table 14.1.

Rahe believed that 150 LCUs within a six-month period indicate that life events will be a contributing factor to a person's subsequent illness. He postulated that there is a gradual build-up of LCUs during the two years preceding a major health

Table 14.1

Rank (1 to 43)	Life Event	Mean Value (LCUs)
8	Fired at work	47
15	Business read-justment	39
16	Change in fi-nancial state	38
18	Change to dif-ferent line of work	36
22	Change in re-sponsibil-ities at work	29
29	Revision of personal habits	24
30	Trouble with boss	23
31	Change in work hours or conditions	20

Source: R. M. Rahe, "Life Crisis and Health Change," in *Psychotropic Drug Response: Advances in Prediction* ed. G. R. Wittenborn (Springfield, IL: Charles C. Thomas, 1969), p. 97.

change. The build-up reaches a maximum level in the last six months before the illness appears.

If a divestiture results in the life events of Table 14.1, the total LCUs would be 256 units. This is well over the illness-creating threshold of 150 units. Even if some of the specific life events do not happen to an individual during or after a divestiture, the perceived threat of the events happening can induce nearly as much stress as their actual occurrence. As Sigmund Freud wrote in 1895, "The uncoupling of associations is always painful."[4]

The stress induced in the managers and employees in a divested segment can lead to stress-induced illnesses as well as the more commonly anticipated decrease in employee morale. Although some investigators have linked these types of life events to very serious human conditions such as depression, suicide, and schizophrenia, most studies have not been able to statistically link the events to these serious illnesses.[5]

B. S. Dohrenwend and B. P. Dohrenwend defined three factors contributing to the levels of stress experienced by an individual. These factors were stressor stimuli, external mediating factors, and internal mediating factors.[6]

STRESSOR STIMULI

Stressor stimuli were described as any events that produce stress. This can occur by the disruption or the threat of disruption of an individual's activities. Sherif and Sherif studied the formation of groups and competition between them. They found increased hostility following the creation of competing groups. Group members perceived the nongroup members as outside of their group and a potential threat to their well-being. The hostility manifested itself by negative sterotyping of the competing group's members, less favorable appraisal of out-group performance, a cutting off of initial friendships without side-group members, overt aggression toward the out-group, and physical separation of the groups.[7] In the situation of a corporate divestiture, this type of hostility can develop between the parent and divested segment if the divestiture is not handled with managerial finesse and consideration.

Stressor stimuli can be expressed by the parent corporation toward the divested component or it can be directed back toward the parent if the divestiture is perceived as a form of rejection. G. Allport listed three levels of out-group rejection. They are verbal rejection, discrimination, and physical attack.[8] Verbal rejection is an expression of animosity and may appear between individuals or indirectly between groups of parent and segment employee groups. Discrimination in the case of divestiture would be the perceived unequal treatment during the divestiture. Physical attack would refer to written or actual forms of attack on the products or services provided by one of the involved corporations. Any of these stimuli can create high levels of stress.

EXTERNAL MEDIATORS

The second factor dealing with the effects of stress on a human is called external mediators by J. Moritsugu and S. Sue.[9] These are the environmental factors that help an individual successfully deal with stress. One such mediator is the social support system. A social system can provide emotional and material support that can lighten the burden imposed by the stress. Involvement with community activities, sharing with peers in the same occupation, neighborhood support, discussing the situation with a marriage partner, and the availability of economic benefits during the stressful period are external mediators found valuable during times of corporate divestiture. The support systems, however, must be used to be effective. Their presence alone does not guarantee successful mediation; the individuals involved have to perceive their value and employ them to be useful.

Support groups organized by the parent company would provide the soon-to-be divested employees with suggestions and help as they cope with the new business environment. Employees of the divested segment would have others, both in the segment and the parent company, with which to share the stressful situation. Aid would be available to the members of the divested segment to help in finding solutions to the stress produced by the parent company's decision to divest.

INTERNAL MEDIATORS

Another mediator during stressful periods are those internal variables that influence the perceived view of the external events and aid the individual to adapt to the situation. How the individual perceives the event of segment divestiture and the resulting affect on the individual depends on the personal attributes of the individual. Personal characteristics of self-commitment, vigorousness, and meaningfulness of one's life are internal mediators important to dealing with stress induced by divesting corporations. If these factors are weak or non-existent in an individual, physical illness has been found to significantly increase.[10]

Members of the diveseted segment's work force may assimilate the attitude of the parent corporation's management, particularly in the parent's decision of divestiture. If the parent has communicated a feeling of limited segment worth, the segment's employees may also internalize that viewpoint. A resulting negative self-image can offset morale gains made in a formal corporate program attempting to prepare the affected employees for the divestiture. This combination of external and internal actions can lead to frustration and mental disturbance.[11]

Some people blame those adversely affected by the internal stimuli with "It's their own fault!" However, Moritsugu and Sue state that it's the interaction with society that creates the "victim's" internal vulnerability.[12] Ecological models for developing divestiture strategies to deal with the stress of the particular divestiture situation may be one way of preparing the divested segment's employees for the induced stress.

If a person feels helpless, fleeing from the situation is often not an available action for the individual. M. Seligman found that a person feeling extreme helplessness tends to passively accept the adverse stimulation, even when action to end the adverse stimulation is available.[13]

When the distance between the individual's perception of his/her working situation and the corporation controlling the divestiture becomes substantial, the individual may feel disenfranchised with a loss of adhesion to the employer. If may grow to an alienation from society in general and lead to serious antisocial behavior. Feelings of unpredictability in divestiture situations can weaken the ability of the employees to deal with the stress of the corporate restructuring.

DIVESTITURE AND STRESS SUMMATION

Divestiture stress has components that affect individuals in different ways and to varying degrees. Psychologists have developed a Social Readjustment Rating Scale to measure the separate components and estimate the potential impact on an individual. A total of 150 scale units may lead to a stress-induced illness.

Stress stimuli are any events that may produce stress. In a divestiture, competing groups for divided assets, markets, or business can induce stress in managers and workers alike. External mediators are the environmental factors that help a person deal with stress. A social support system and involvement with outside activities are helpful external stress mediators. Internal mediators are based on the perceived view of the stressful events. The perception of the divestiture in the minds of the employees of the parent and divested segment may aid or increase the stressful situation.

15

Psychological Effects of Divestiture

When divestiture becomes the business option, corporate employees may experience many psychological problems related to the divestiture activity. The most common factor is the increased stress level present in most divestiture situations. The effects of stress may include:

1. Organizational confusion
2. Managerial and employee anxiety
3. Corporate paralysis
4. Protective defense mechanisms
5. Preventive measures

ORGANIZATIONAL CONFUSION

As a corporate separation nears, managers and employees often long for pre-divestiture days. The intermittent longing for keeping the corporation intact may continue for a year or more after the divestiture before it begins to fade. This was found in a parallel situation of separation between a husband and wife.[1]

E. M. Hetherington et al. determined that a separated couple predominantly experience a chaotic lifestyle after the separation.[2] Corporations can experience the same phenomena. Communication channels once open no longer exist. Accessibility to executives and financial resources change. Marketing policies, financing arrangements, promotion practices, quality standards, and technical support may change or cease to exist. Organizational confusion can suddenly appear. If it does and a concerted effort is made to bring it under control, it may take as long as two years after the divestiture to renew a stable organizational structure.

MANAGERIAL AND EMPLOYEE ANXIETY

Although stress-induced anxiety has been discussed, other sources of anxiety exist in a divestiture. The negative connotation of separation, whether in marriage or in corporations, is still present in the United States. Stable relationships in both marriage and business are defined by many as the keystones of a successful economy. This concept inhibits divestiture as it does divorce.

Many employees become emotionally dependent on the parent company. Corporate divestiture threatens the dependency. Divestiture has been defined as a process that destroys the corporate entity and creates trauma in the business segment. S. Gettleman and J. Markowitz state that the destruction connotation in divorce has come from the analogy of divorce and death.[3] Corporate divestiture may suffer under the same analogy.

Psychological literature on divorce often contains the bias that emotional pathology and personal tragedy are the inevitable component of a divorce.[4] A. J. Cherlin points out that the process of divorce can benefit the adults that complete it because it may free them from the tensions of an unhappy marriage.[5] Divestiture also can relieve the tensions and anxieties that develop when a mismatch occurs within a corporate business.

In the past, the business literature has helped to reinforce the concept that divestiture often results from a partial or complete business failure. Recently, a more positive attitude has appeared that recognizes that corporate divestiture can result in two successful companies rather than a larger but unhealthy corporation. The appearance of "losers" in a divestiture is giving way to the term redirecting corporate efforts.

CORPORATE PARALYSIS

Anxiety can build to a point in an individual or group such that important and necessary decisions will not be made. In some situations, managers will concentrate on details in order to avoid major decisions. Executives may leave the office for any minor reason and be unavailable for important business questions. Employees may miss work because of claimed sick leave. Work may significantly slow because everyone seems to spend most of their work periods discussing the upcoming divestiture. The entire corporation appears to be busy, but no decisions are made. A case of corporate paralysis has set in and may be terminal if it is not quickly reversed.

An alert management of the parent or segment company must exercise leadership and take charge of the situation. A positive atmosphere of "Let's get on with life" has to be instilled. The importance of preparing the segment for a timely divestiture has to be forcefully restated in action and words. Recognition of the stress of the situation and the individual differences of dealing with stress should make management aware of the need for communicating the status and ongoing stages of the divestiture. The corporation has to awaken from its paralysis and deal with the divestiture.

Anxiety can have benefits. It can alert individuals and prepare them for coping with their changing environment in an effective fashion. It can make individuals more perceptive of their surroundings. Mild anxiety can act as a motivator in increasing job performance. If it becomes intense, job performance usually declines.

However, a rigidity in one's perception of the environment can result. Generalizations are made about adverse conditions and extended beyond rational limits. Poor performance also may be a negative product of anxious business situations. If an employee is preoccupied with his or her potential job evaluation, then a poor performance may be the product, although the employee had always performed well in the past. A third negative effect of anxiety may be an avoidance of what they know they should be doing. An individual may avoid a work situation because it may cause him or her future increased levels of anxiety. This may be present even if the employee has performed the work successfully before the threat of divestiture appeared. All of these negative reactions to anxiety can be eliminated by significant reductions in the anxiety-producing cause.

PROTECTIVE DEFENSE MECHANISMS

Individual methods used by management or employees to deal with the stress-induced anxiety were described by Freud as defense mechanisms to protect the individual from the anxiety. They are:

1. *Repression*. Unwanted thoughts, feelings, or impulses are unconsciously barred from the conscious mind. These repressed thoughts may be revealed by slips of the tongue, the choice of humor, or the dreams a person has.

2. *Suppression*. Suppression operates on the conscious level. It is a voluntary effort to put something out of one's mind. The person who refuses to think about the divestiture because it is too threatening is using this defense.

3. *Rationalization*. An attempt to provide justification for thoughts, feelings, or behaviors that make the individual uncomfortable. An employee may quit with the rationalization that he doesn't like to work in the particular organization rather than admit that his job performance was not adequate.

4. *Identification*. Identification can be used to obtain gratification that is otherwise unavailable or to increase self-esteem. An individual can identify with an organization to offset feelings of inadequacy. If a divestiture reduces these individual identifications with a successful unit and assigns it a label of "troubled" organization, the individuals employed in the unit may also feel they are inadequate.

5. *Projection*. Projection involves attributing one's own feelings and motives to others to protect oneself from anxiety causing situations. Persons believe that others behave as they do for the same reasons. It is difficult for some employees to understand that not all employees feel the same way about a divestiture and the stress it may induce as they do. Isn't everyone anxious about the changing situation? Isn't everyone worried about their careers in the divested unit? Isn't everyone concerned?

6. *Reaction Formation*. An individual may repress one set of feelings and overemphasize another set. A person may repress the feelings of job anxiety with an emphasis on the positive opportunities a divestiture may bring.

7. *Compensation*. A person may compensate for a perceived psychological or physical defect by overcompensating for the defect. A shy person may compensate for it by intimidation of others. A depressed person may constantly act overjoyed at the situation.

8. *Displacement*. An individual may take an action toward someone who did not contribute to making the stressful situation. A husband involved in a stressful divestiture may displace his feelings of a loss of control in his job situation by emotional or physical abuse of his wife.

9. *Fantasy*. Fantasy may be resorted to by individuals when they are dissatisfied with a job situation. They may attempt to create a world of fantasy that is more satisfying and enjoyable than the one in which they find themselves.

10. *Substitution*. An employee may substitute a successful activity for the perceived unsuccessful one in the divesting unit.[6]

Everyone uses some form of defense mechanism to protect themselves in anxiety producing environments. Most of them do not interfere with job performance. The danger lies in the excessive use of these mechanisms. The defense techniques may reduce the anxiety in a person's mind, but it does nothing about the source of the anxiety. It often can delay the adaptation to the changed business situation during and after the divestiture.

PREVENTIVE MEASURES

Communications dealing with the divestiture situation should be put in place immediately when a divestiture is determined. Stress always will be present in the divested segment's personnel. Increasing the self-image and worth of the employees, helping the divested segment improve their economic future, building a sense of community in the divested segment, strengthening support groups within the company and outside the business, and being actively attentive to detect excessive signs of stress are steps that can be employed by both the parent and segment management to aid the segment's employees to successfully deal with the stress of the divestiture.

Employees of the divested segment may feel that they personally and collectively have failed the parent corporation in making the segment a business success. The employees need to feel that their self-worth as productive workers is valuable. If their productivity was a primary issue in the divestiture, other personal employee characteristics and abilities need to be identified and emphasized in communications to the divested work force. The strengths of the employees need to be emphasized if the divested segment is to have a chance to be successful on its own. If the parent determines that the subsidiary work force is not worthy or capable of success, the subsidiary should have been liquidated and its assets sold piecemeal or reassigned to other corporate components.

By providing business advice or other intangible support, the parent corporation can reduce the stress in the divested segment employees as it helps the new independent corporation be freestanding. The transfer of sales accounts, selected personnel, trademarks, patents, and other business items may substantially add to the probability of success of the new corporation.

The segment employees probably associated themselves with the parent corporation. P. Selznick in 1943 singled out informal organizational structures as the primary instrument for modifying organizational goals and policies under conditions of changing situational demands.[7] By building a segment esprit de corps with company-sponsored segment identified athletic teams, community activities, employee benefit items, and facilities identification, management can begin the process of constructing a sense of community within the segment that is not directly identified with the parent corporation.

Support groups have been recognized as valuable aids in reducing stress. The creation and use of supportive relationships are important in dealing with stress and should include friends, family, acquaintances, and coworkers. Although there isn't a "one best way" stress-management technique, individuals must deal with stress in a manner in which they are most comfortable.[8] In research with a particular type of work position, personal care attendants, Atkins, Meyer, and Smith found that the attendants themselves suggested support groups as important in aiding during stressful periods.[9] The support group is beneficial because it involves self-disclosure and feedback. Individuals have the opportunity to be open and honest about their feelings on particular issues or situations. Group members should possess the ability to develop mutually supportive relationships with their colleagues.[10] Employees should be permitted group participation during the work day. Such time should be considered as "goof-off" time, but should be viewed as an effective way to combat the stress from divestiture.[11]

Management has to be alert for the signs of excessive stress during the time the divestiture first becomes a subject of conversation to the time the divestiture is complete and the business situation indicates the divested segment is successful. As J. Adler and M. Gosnell found in their 1980 research, handling stressful situations depends on the attitude of the employees toward their job. Those who are dissatisfied show an increased risk of developing hypertension. The intensity of the stress appears to be less important than the way it is handled by the individual. Handling it poorly makes stress a factor in causing illness.[12]

PSYCHOLOGICAL EFFECTS SUMMATION

Divestiture can be one of the most stressful experiences in a corporations's existence. Effects on the corporation may be in the form of organizational confusion, managerial and employee anxiety, and, in extreme cases, a complete paralysis of the corporation. Individuals may use many different defense mechanisms to shield themselves from the adverse effects of divestiture anxiety. Management has to be aware of the effects of stress induced by a divestiture and exercise leadership in moving the divestiture to a successful conclusion.

Different techniques are available including helping the employees improve their self-image, helping the segment improve their economic future, building an identity within the segment, strengthening segment employee support groups, and being sensitive to the signs of excessive stress.

16

Divestiture Considerations

Techniques used in divestitures are based on the analysis and expertise of the individuals participating in the corporate restructuring decisions. Overall considerations have to be drawn from different sources. The considerations and sources include:

1. Divestiture timing
2. Internal sources
3. External sources
4. Planning steps

DIVESTITURE TIMING

The timing of the divestiture transaction is as important as any important business exchange. Areas of potential timing irritation include the delays in finding a buyer and closing the transaction, and the prolonged uncertainty of some managers and employees. Once the divestiture decision is made, management usually wants the divestiture to be completed as quickly as possible. This is particularly true if the segment is an operating cash drain. If the offering is on the market too long, potential buyers may become skeptical about the value of the segment, key personnel may leave, employee morale may fall, internal information leaks may develop along with free flying rumors, and the result may be an extensive lowering of the selling price.

As with any complex business transaction dealing with significant changes in the corporation, the more people involved, the more difficult it is to keep the negotiations private. Planning before the offering of the segment regardless of the divestiture method used is of the utmost importance.

INTERNAL SOURCES

In preparation for the divestiture procedure and during the actual divestiture transaction, management requires professional aid in pulling the necessary information together for effective negotiations and carrying out the many details required. In the first place, divestiture requires top management access and participation. The operating head of the divested segment, however, is generally *not* considered the best person to actively participate in the financial planning and negotiations of the divestiture. No matter how it is dressed up, divestiture is often perceived as an admission of failure.

The operating head may be identified formally or informally as contributing to the failure. This destroys the objectivity or perceived objectivity of the present operating management in dealing with the divestiture procedure. The entire divestiture process is generally a thankless task that brings no obvious future benefits to the divestiture team. The internal management team is often composed of a senior manager, preferably not directly involved with the divested segment, a financial analyst, usually from the finance or accounting departments, a tax person, and someone familiar with stock issues. The last member is often from the treasurer's office. Infrequently, the team contains a marketing or expert public affairs member.[1]

Because of the infrequent nature of divestitures for most corporations, top management often turns to external sources for help in planning and implementing a divestiture procedure. Finding a buyer, after analyzing the apparent value of the segment, is perceived by many as a special skill held by merchant banks and acquisition/divestiture brokers. Large accounting firms have participated to a greater extent than in prior years, but conflict of interest and possible liability concerns have made some firms move very cautiously into the divestiture consulting business.

EXTERNAL SOURCES

Services provided by external sources are similar to those of internal management teams. In some situations, the parent divesting company may proceed with both an internal team and employ outside special skills or a complete duplicate group. The outside group becomes particularly valuable in helping find a potential buyer and organizing financing for the buyer.

The independent certified public accountant (CPA) can make a particularly valuable contribution to the seller in a divestiture situation. Although there are no authoritative professional standards for the conduct of a predivestiture review, procedures should be agreed upon between the CPA and the client before the review and they should be based on the use of professional judgment.

The evaluation of specific account types, elements, or items in many cases are covered by authoritative sources, but the expressing of an opinion is still based on the professional judgment of the CPA. The CPA has to keep in mind that he/she has some degree of responsibility to all parties involved in the negotiations, not just the seller.

Specifically, the CPA may assist the client in preparing the divestiture plan with an evaluation of alternative divestiture methods. He/she may search for a buyer of the segment and later structure the actual divestiture transaction to meet the objectives of the seller. Of course, the CPA is a valuable source of advice during the actual negotiations. Aid in separating control systems and redesigning internal reporting procedures is a necessary but often overlooked function that can be effectively performed by the CPA firm. The valuation of inventories, accounts receivable, and deferred tax amounts as well as verifying the historical costs of fixed assets and related depreciation are items that the CPA is ably prepared to perform. A sales prospectus may be prepared by the CPA to interest potential buyers.[2]

The question of independence must be constantly evaluated and active participation in the negotiations may be considered as impairing that status.

The legal environment of such complex business transactions as divestitures requires the close involvement of legal experts. They are absolutely necessary throughout the procedures because the potential legal disasters far outweigh most operating losses of unsuccessful segments. The drafting of transfer documents and understanding of the laws dealing with the transfer of corporate ownership are necessary if lawsuits are to be avoided.

PLANNING STEPS

When divestiture of a business segment is the alternative chosen, C. J. Clarke and F. Gall recommend following a six-step approach to a planned divestment. Several of the early steps are completed before the final decision to divest is made. The steps are:[3]

1. Establish the need for divestiture. Establish the exact scale and nature of the need to divest. Is it a lack of strategic fit, the wrong risk profile, inappropriate cash flow, or is the segment outside the central mission of the corporation? Has it failed to achieve an adequate profit performance?

2. Conduct an internal review of those business segments subject to divestiture. Review the internal activities and resources of the candidates. Review the economic relationships of the candidate segments to the rest of the corporation. Narrow the number of divestiture candidates.

3. Conduct an external review of the final candidates for divestiture. An external review is prepared from the standpoint of how an outsider or external viewer sees and values the divestiture segments. The external review may be conducted by the internal corporate staff, but it reviews the external effects and factors affecting the possible divestitures. Review sales, market trends, and profit forecasts of both the divestiture candidate segments and the corporation as a whole. Compare the return on investment and profitability with and without the divestiture candidates. Highlight the

competitive strengths of the corporation. Identify and evaluate the important business players in the market.

4. Evaluate the options. How should the divestiture be conducted? Should it be done exclusively by the corporate staff or is outside expertise needed? Should the divestiture segments be spun off, closed down, or sold as a going concern? What should be the selling price?

5. Qualify the buyers. Who should be approached as a potential buyer? How should the potential buyers be approached and by whom? What forms of payment would be acceptable? How much publicity should be used and when?

6. Close the divestiture. Develop the sales strategy, develop negotiating tactics and negotiate with the potential buyers. Assure the financial soundness of any offers. Measure each offer against the needs of the corporation. Assure that employee and public relations remain sound throughout the negotiations.

DIVESTITURE TECHNIQUES SUMMATION

The timing is important to close the divestiture transaction. Management support activities for the divestiture analysis can be developed internally or externally or a mixture of both. An example of the specific planning steps from a Clarke and Gall study used in preparing for a divestiture has been provided.

17

Specific Divestiture Techniques

Specific divestiture techniques employed vary from the simple to the complex. They include:

1. Spin-off to stockholders
2. Segment sale for assets
3. Leveraged buyout considering both secured and unsecured lending
4. Employee stock ownership plans
5. Royalty trusts

SPIN-OFF TO STOCKHOLDERS

A spin-off to stockholders has become one of the most popular divestiture methods used by corporations. A spin-off of a wholly owned entity to stockholders as a freestanding and separate corporation can be accomplished by assigning the ownership of the subsidiary to present stockholders of the parent corporation, sometimes with offerings to the public. The spin-off provides the profit center entity with assets, liabilities, and its own equity base. Although in theory the stockholders of the parent corporation are no better off after the spin-off than before, the marketplace often places a higher value on the two separate business entities than it did on the two combined units. One of the dangers for the parent corporation in a spin-off is that the market may lower its valuation of the parent if the spun-off entity is perceived as a key operation. Stock spin-offs generally are accomplished as tax-free distributions to owners because they are exchanging one indication of corporate ownership for another of similar value. In 1987 CBS Inc. favored a spin-off of its record unit to its stockholders rather that an outright sale to Sony Corp. of Japan because the spin-off was tax-free to CBS, but a $600 million tax liability would incur if the record unit were sold to Sony.[1]

Accounting Principles Board Opinion No. 29, *Accounting For Nonmonetary Transactions*, applies to spin-offs because spin-offs involve nonreciprocal transfers of nonmonetary assets from an enterprise to its owners. The distribution should be based on the recorded amounts of the nonmonetary asset distributed. The board holds that because the distribution was prorata to the present stockholders, the overall nature of the total businesses is the same after the spin-off as it was before. This transaction is recorded at book values and no gains are recognized. Losses, however, are always recognized when sustained.

Involuntary spin-offs are usually the result of a complaint filed by a federal or state regulatory agency. Voluntary spin-offs also may be made in response to regulatory conditions. Separating regulatory from unregulated businesses may result in a corporate subsidiary spin-off. A number of involuntary spin-offs resulted from the Bank Holding Company Act of 1969, which required companies whose business was not principally banking to divest themselves of ownership or control of commercial banks.[2] The largest spin-off was in a regulated industry, interstate communications. AT&T's 22 operating companies were spun-off into seven holding companies in compliance with a federal court order.

Research by Miles and Rosenfeld has shown that just the announcement of a spin-off has a positive influence on the stock price of the parent. The relative increase in share price is greater for large spin-offs than for small ones. A sample of 55 voluntary spin-offs show the positive effect of announcements on shareholder wealth and that, on the average, the announcements precede a period of abnormally positive stock price changes.[3] Rosenfeld followed the price changes further. He compared the stock price effects of a spin-off announcement to that of a segment sell-off announcement. He found the spin-off positive effects outperformed the changes of the sell-off announcement. He also found that the economic gains to the shareholders of the selling and acquiring companies are nearly identical, suggesting that the divestiture decision is perceived by both investor groups as a positive net present value transaction. Although the sell-off may bring a larger inflow of cash flow to the parent than a spin-off, the more favorable differential tax situation with a spin-off may cause the more favorable spin-off stock market effect.[4] When a corporation is considering a spin-off, corporate officers should obtain a private IRS letter ruling on the stockholder tax consequences before proceeding with the spin-off.

One corporate officer remarked about their recent spin-off, "By spinning off from RLC Corporation, we are telling the world that we are now mature and are able to stand on our own financially. It's a way of saying, 'Look at us, we're growing!' " Speculative fever may not be rewarded as fast as anticipated for many spun-off businesses. Few spin-offs produce spectacular results. A subsidiary that is buried under the reputation of the parent may not be given the attention it deserves in the stock market. A spun-off company is tracked by experts in the new segment industry rather than the industry of the parent corporation. They may not be familiar with the past record of the now independent business segment, and be slow to react to favorable operating reports.[5]

In a few cases, the parent has benefited immediately after a spin-off. After a 1983 spin-off of its containerized freight subsidiary Sea-Land Industries Investments, J. R. Reynolds Industries' price earnings ratio increased from 7.5 to 9.5 until it more closely resembled the peer group of consumer products companies which Reynolds then more closely resembled.[6]

Spin-offs are not cost-free. Besides the internal staff time required to analyze and prepare the divestiture, underwriting commissions on a public securities issue are a short-term, out-of-pocket expense. Commissions on a spin-off may be 5 percent of the proceeds where fees on a sale are generally 1 percent or less. Also massive documentation for both methods is required. If the corporation can absorb the expense, the rewards to the stockholders can be significant. Three major studies have found positive share-price reactions after the spin-offs. This indicates that the stock market may evaluate the sum of a corporation's parts as greater than the whole.[7]

An example of the complexity of the businesses spun-off from a major corporation can be determined from the Ametek Inc. divestiture. In March 1988 an announcement was made that the corporation would spin-off several of its divisions into one separate company. This would allow the parent to concentrate on the precision technology business. The divisions included aluminum extrusion, plastics, heat transfer equipment, and undersea work vehicles. Their combined sales amounted to 30 percent and 5 percent of net income for Ametek in 1987. The new company is said to expect stable earnings and substantial sales. No name was chosen nor a stock distribution plan to Ametek stockholders announced.[8]

SEGMENT SALE FOR ASSETS

Selling a business segment for cash is probably the most straightforward method of divestiture. An exchange of other assets, such as land, manufacturing, or distribution facilities, may be more complicated than an exchange for cash, but it is conceptually the same. The principal attraction, of course, is that the seller gains a liquid or near-liquid asset in exchange for primarily nonliquid, possibly loss-producing, assets.

Determining the true value of the net assets sold and the value of assets received can be a difficult task. The book value of the assets may be misleading. A method used by security analysts but scorned by accountants is determining the fair market value rather than the historical costs used on the financial statements. Substituting liquidation value for the book value of the assets provides a minimum value for a segment. A common stock is unlikely to sell for less than the liquidation value of the assets for any extended time. At some point, the stock market catches up. On the other hand, a money manager analyzes the balance sheets and reconstructs them in accordance with economic reality rather than with accounting conventions. Then an estimated market value can be assigned to each asset category. The sum of the newly valued assets less the liabilities equals the restated net worth. The restated net worth is an estimate of market worth of the segment.

LEVERAGED BUYOUT

In recent years the leveraged buyout (LBO) by the corporation's employees, management, or external buyers has become popular in divestiture circles. Individual employees, employee groups, management, or external buyers may borrow funds to purchase the divested business segment and provide notes payable or the shares in the new divested corporation as collateral for the monies necessary to purchase the segment. With inside buyers groups, divestiture negotiations can be difficult because of the familiarity with the situation. When insiders or key personnel are involved, questions such as conflict of interest and adequate valuation to the selling stockholders become more important considerations than if the same divestiture agreement were completed with an outside party.

In 1988 Ross Johnson, president of RJR Nabisco, led a group of top managers into offering shareholders first $17.6 billion and then $22.7 billion to take the corporation private. The leveraged buyout would allow the group of managers to take complete control of RJR after which he planned to sell off the corporation's food brands. RJR's 1987 revenues were $15.8 billion. The managers expected the value of their investment to increase to $200 billion or more after the transaction was complete. The LBO was quickly superseded by proposals of an investment banker and an investment group. The reaction to the Johnson offer was loud throughout the financial community. Economist Robert Reich of Harvard said, "This is the sort of excess that investment bankers have worried about for years because it so clearly exposes the greed and rapaciousness of so many of these takeovers." The managing partner of a Wall Street arbitrage firm added, "Do I sense fear? Yes. At some point there is going to be a rebellion against greed."[9] The stockholders refused to sell to Johnson and his group of corporate managers.

Future earnings in the divested segment are used to retire the new debt. Secured financing is provided when the assets of the acquired operation are used to collateralize the debt. Any difference between the value of the asset collateral and the purchase price is usually covered by an equity investment by the purchasing group and/or the notes payable held by the seller. The leveraged buyout leaves the acquired operating entity with a greater than traditional debt-to-equity ratio. Ratios relating to return on assets are distorted because interest costs will be relatively high and earnings relatively low, thereby driving down the return on assets.

For example, Burlington Industries Inc. was bought out in 1987 by a group headed by the New York investment banking firm of Morgan Stanley & Co. Before the buyout, the debt to common equity ratio was 0.4 to 1. After the buyout, the ratio became 29.8 to 1. A prospectus issued in 1988 warns that the new indebtedness bears interest at higher average rates than before the buyout. With anticipated levels of operations, the company does not expect that it would be able to generate sufficient cash flow from operations to service its debt without selling certain assets. In the fourth quarter of 1987, Burlington lost $25.3 million, although there was an increase in earnings from operations. It was blamed on $66.1 million in interest expense.

A June 21, 1984, editorial in the *Wall Street Journal* listed another danger with LBOs:

If a buyout is so heavily leveraged that there is intense pressure for cash flow, there is a danger that the company will simply be run into the ground. The temptation is toward deferred maintenance and research, skimping on middle management and other forms of economizing. The danger is especially great when companies fall into the hands of professional leveragers who take their cut up front and when managers have very little of their own money involved.

In the same time period, John Shad, chairman of the Securities and Exchange Commission, wrote in the June 8, 1984, *Wall Street Journal* concerning LBOs, the use of the corporation's own assets, and the creation of substantial debt: "To do so, it is usually necessary to dedicate such cash flows to future debt service, rather than to the replacement of aging plant and declining oil or other reserves. . . . The leveraging up of American enterprise will magnify the adverse consequences of the next recession or the next significant rise in interest rates."

The liberalization of investing standards is attributed by L. H. Clark, Jr., and A. L. Malabre, Jr., to the fact that the United States has not had a depression since the 1930s and businessmen respond by saying, "Why should we be worried if our credit rating goes from A to BBB? The tax code encourages debt because interest is deductible and dividends are not."[10] A leveraged buyout is an attempt to buy time while gaining control of the segment corporation. Time and the related earnings stream are necessary to retire the newly assumed debt. The buyer hopes to use the tangible or intangible value-added factors to elevate the divested segment to a higher level of profitability and cash flow within a shorter time than could have been done by the prior owner. This may be done by:

1. Emphasizing cash flow rather than taxable income;
2. Eliminating excessive parent corporation management fees and salaries;
3. Selling excess low-earning assets to raise cash;
4. Freeing management from restrictions by the parent corporation's controls;
5. Exercising the opportunity to penetrate new markets that prior owners ignored; and
6. Improving inefficient operations.[11]

Secured Lending

A secured transaction normally involves three parties—the buyer, the seller, and the financing source. A secured debt financier is concerned with collateral coverage and with debt service coverage rather than the financial strength and ability to amortize the debt principal. The lender is interested in both cash flows and the downside collateral coverage. The lender is concentrating on the first 12 months after the leveraged buyout

because it is normally the critical period of the segment operating independently. The inflationary environment of the 1970s
encouraged secured financing since fixed asset collateral would
actually appreciate with time. In addition, buyers would repay
borrowings at a future date with devalued dollars. With the
prime rate lower than the inflationary rate, buyers were getting
essentially free financing.[12]

Unsecured Lending

Unsecured lending normally involves some combination of
venture capital, subordinated debt, generally with an equity
conversion feature, and senior debt. The total equals the purchase price. This form of buyout is often referred to as a cash
flow leveraged buyout. The successful leveraged buyout usually requires the participation of management, lenders, equity
investors, lawyers, accountants, and financial advisors. This form
of financing is more complex than secured borrowing because
each level of financing normally comes from a different lending
or investment source. Lenders and investors recognize that they
take a substantial equity risk with a highly leveraged, long-term
unsecured financing. Therefore, they generally insist on sharing in the company's expected future success by participating
in the equity ownership of the divested segment. It enables the
buyer to finance a purchase price well in excess of the company's book value or real asset value. Long-term lenders and equity investors are not basing their financing decision on asset
valuation. The significant debt service requirements in an unsecured leveraged buyout add importance to cash flow fore-
casting, profit center management, pricing decisions, and competitors' actions. There is little value in closely monitoring specific
assets over time. Since security is not critical to the investors,
leaving the assets of a highly leveraged company unencum-
bered occasionally enhances the firm's ability to obtain favorable terms on trade credit. Investors look closely at the consis-
tency of historical earnings and the stability of profit margins.
Investors eagerly agree to management's ownership of a substantial part of the company for what is usually a very small
percentage of the purchase price.[13]

Whether a LBO is secured or unsecured, Barry and Stratton listed characteristics they thought were highly desirable for the long-term success of a corporation subject to a leveraged buyout. They are:[14]

1. Book value of assets lower than the current fair market value
2. Low existing debt
3. Strong earnings record
4. Experienced management staying with the business
5. Stable growth record in noncyclical business
6. Quality tangible assets
7. Low level of future capital requirements
8. Excess assets, which can be sold to generate cash
9. Excess cash to help finance acquisition
10. A diversified customer base

EMPLOYEE STOCK OWNERSHIP PLANS

In the late 1950s the employee stock ownership plan (ESOP) was developed and, in the early 1970s, given the name by Louis Kelso. It enabled employees to buy the business with payments made from their share of pretax corporate earnings without payroll deductions or the investment of their personal savings. The corporation could give the employees an added benefit without putting the corporation at a competitive wage scale disadvantage. An employee stock ownership trust, the ESOP administrative body, was required to invest the employees' set-aside share of the corporate earnings in the securities of the corporation. This modified stock purchase plan eventually received a favorable United States Treasury ruling to permit the plans to borrow and then purchase employer stock. As the assets of the company were paid for, the employee stock ownership plan and the employees became the owners without the earnings used to retire the debt being subject to personal income taxes. Corporations can deduct from taxable income any dividends paid to an ESOP, which is an attractive way for a corporation to raise tax deductible common equity. Presently, this same concept has been classified as a stock bonus or retirement plan and is being applied to divestitures. When an ESOP borrows to purchase the common stock of an employer corporation, the lender is now required to pay tax on only half of the interest income from the loan (Tax Reform Act of 1984, Sections 542 and 543). Contributions paid by an employer to an ESOP are deductible, up to 25 percent of the payroll (Internal Revenue Code, Section 415, paragraph 19,566). In addition, there is a tax credit on contributions, limited to 0.75 percent (three-fourths of 1 percent) of the annual payroll. The tax-deduction benefit is in addition to the benefit of the low interest cost that may be made possible by the favorable tax treatment received by the lender. As the debt is retired, the shares of stock held by the trustee are credited to the participants' accounts in the ESOP.[15]

The leveraged ESOP may lift employee morale and enable the corporation to pay less in direct wage compensation because of the accumulating wealth in the ESOP. Unions or groups of employees are forming such plans to purchase segments of the business.

The ESOPs met a number of objectives. They could:[16]

1. Raise capital
2. Recapture taxes
3. Improve individual estate liquidity
4. Retire outstanding stock shares
5. Provide a market for closely held stock
6. Discourage unionization
7. Buy out dissident stockholders
8. Be used to acquire other companies
9. Be used to combat tender offers
10. Broaden the appeal of existing unions
11. Shelter excess accumulated earnings
12. Refinance existing debt
13. Maximize IRS investment tax credit
14. Be used for segment divestiture
15. Purchase key man insurance

Leveraged ESOPS have become very popular. In the case of the Soo Line Corporation, management held talks with union representatives about the acquisition of all or part of the company through an employee stock ownership plan. The union represents 4,000 employees. Labor officials raised the possibility during discussions over a wide range of ways to reduce the line's labor costs and improve its cost structure. The stock price of the Soo Line jumped on the NYSE.[17]

A consulting firm, the National Center for Employee Ownership in Oakland, California, estimates that ESOPs borrowed $5.5 billion in 1987, quadrupling their 1986 borrowings. In 1987 approximately 300,000 employees acquired a share of ownership in their companies through the plans. Where ESOPs bought most or all of a corporation, $4.5 billion was borrowed by the plans, which equaled 15 percent of the total committed to leveraged buyouts in 1987. In 1986 leveraged ESOPs accounted for 3 percent of the total funds committed to leveraged buyouts. Leveraged ESOPs are becoming a significant factor in buyout proposals. Some of the major leveraged ESOPs begun in 1987 were:[18]

Avis Inc.	$1.75 billion
HealthTrust Inc.	$1.7 billion
Austin Industries Inc.	$300 million
Norcal	$82 million

Under consideration in 1987:

J. P. Stevens & Co. Inc.	$700 million
DynCorp	$200 million

ROYALTY TRUSTS

The royalty trust concept was developed in the oil and gas industry as a specialized segment spin-off. A portion of a corporation's oil and gas producing reserves are transferred to the shareholders. These assets can no longer be claimed by purchasers of the parent firm because they are held in trust for the stockholders. They have been used as a method for the parent company to avoid a takeover bid by other corporations because many of the corporation's valuable assets were no longer owned by the corporation. If the trust is created by distributing properties to the shareholders as a dividend, under current law, the corporation would not generally pay any tax on the difference between the cost of the property and the current value.

The ability to distribute the properties without recognizing gain is very important to the economics of the overall transaction. The fundamental objective is to recognize a net profit interest from a producing property and transfer ownership of this property directly to the shareholders. The advantage is that the shareholder can receive direct income without first being taxed as part of the corporation's income. Although it may look much like a dividend, it is considered royalty income and the corporate tax on that income has been eliminated. The shareholder will then expect a lower actual dividend payment because he or she is also receiving a royalty income. A royalty interest is required to permit the trust to qualify as a fixed investment trust. A royalty trust is not subject to federal taxes and is required to pay out 90 percent of its earnings as dividends to stockholders. For a corporation with a large number of individual shareholders, royalty trusts are much more attractive where there is no accumulated taxable income and the distribution will be treated as a return of capital. The trust cannot have a working interest in the producing asset. As a fixed investment trust, the trust itself pays no tax. The beneficiaries or divested unit holders are directly taxed on all income received. The income received by the unit holder retains its character as royalty and may be eligible for depletion.[19] Although some royalty trusts are found in the oil and gas industry, no other industries have chosen this method to transfer ownership of a business segment to the shareholders.

SPECIFIC DIVESTITURE TECHNIQUES SUMMATION

The stock market reaction to divestitures is similar regardless of the type of divestiture method. A study by James Rosenfeld, reported in the December 1984 issue of *The Journal of Finance*, concluded that specific types of divestitures (sell-offs and spin-offs were analyzed) of corporations with comparable financial strength were treated by the stock market in a similar fashion. He found that both divestiture methods were perceived by stockholders as favorable to the parent's net cash flow at the time of the divestiture announcement. This study indicates that the stock market reaction appears to be independent of the divestiture method employed. As indicated in Table 12.1, the market does adjust the stock price later if the divestiture isn't really perceived as favorable for the parent corporation.

All five divestiture techniques have been used successfully in the United States as well as abroad. Royalty trusts are used more infrequently than the other four. Each technique is aimed at a different corporate goal. Spin-offs and royalty trusts leave the present stockholders in control of corporate assets. Sales of corporate assets, employee stock ownership plans, and leveraged buyouts either introduce new owners or the corporation assets are permanently transferred out of the stockholder's control. The methods may be complex or deceptively simple as in the case of some asset sales.

18

Divestiture Directions

When strategic considerations are made in a corporation, divestiture becomes a normal business practice to reshape the direction of the corporation as the goals and objectives change with time. This philosophy views divestiture as a means of company growth and profit enhancement by "pruning out" weak products, assets, or activities, and replacing them with new investments that will earn a higher rate of return and improve earnings per share.[1] Just as employees and executives change with time, the makeup of the corporation components change. The corporation doesn't have to wait until a bankruptcy forces it into restructuring; it can and should be done on a regular basis as the corporation and industry matures. Corporate considerations will include:

1. Divestiture as accepted policy
2. Segment production or divestiture
3. Employees and new owners
4. Antitrust activity
5. Corporate raiders

Divestiture has become part of a healthy, growing, profitable, and successful corporation as well as a way out for an unsuccessful corporation.

DIVESTITURE AS ACCEPTED POLICY

With many companies diversifying piecemeal, they have found it necessary to correct the resulting heterogeneous mixture of components. This requires management time and effort that could be better invested in helping the corporation grow and prosper. Restructuring and the associated divestiture, if necessary, can become a normal part of the corporation's routine. A multiproduct company constantly needs to readjust to new market needs and demands. Divestiture is one method of readjustment just as new product design is another. AMF chairman and CEO Thomas York said, "Restructuring is a continuous way of life in a company that serves as many and as diverse markets as we do and with the number of products that we have. We'll never get to the point where we can say, 'This is it,' and watch the magic growth of the future."[2]

Large divestitures, $1 billion or more, will continue, but more small and medium-size corporations will discover divestitures as an acceptable business alternative, much as bank loans for expansion have become a normal business procedure. As international trade becomes more competitive, old combinations and ways of doing business will not be adequate to compete successfully in the global arena. Corporate international combinations will lead to corporate international separations. Employees and communities will have a more difficult period of adjusting to the rapidly changing business combinations and management changes. Employee allegiance may become more closely associated with a smaller unit within the local operation similar to the recently accepted team concept used in the automobile assembly plant. Top management may become more concerned with the financial structure and performance of the parent corporation and its subsidiaries and leave the detailed control of quality, production levels, sales amounts, and employee selection and promotion to lower and middle management. Many of these shifts are seen in the decentralized decision making that has occurred in corporate America in the 1980s.

In the severe cyclical economics of the 1970s and 1980s, board members increasingly became aware of the need for a corporate strategy. Each corporation had a corporate culture and could conduct some functions well and some less well. The strategic recognition of divestiture required companies to divest businesses that no longer met the long-term strategic requirements of the parent corporation. This is a marked contrast with the emphasis put on diversification during the 1960s. Although growth in sales and market share were attainable by diversification, earnings growth was more elusive.

SEGMENT PRODUCTION OR DIVESTITURE

Business segments are expected to produce the items the corporation expects or be subject to divestiture. As corporations become more earnings conscious, each component will be measured internally to a standard and if it has not met this standard, corrective measures can be expected. In more and more cases, the corporate expectations involve earnings performance. W. R. Grace owns the Herman's Sporting Goods chain, which has been a significant contributor to sales. In the fiscal year of 1985, the chain had sales of $2 billion, which was 28 percent of the entire corporate sales. Earnings, however, were only 10 percent of the company's net income from operations. This was comparable to the 65 percent of earnings provided by the specialty and agricultural chemical units. The corporate management decided to sell its 660-store sporting goods chain because of inadequate profit performance and use the proceeds to repurchase their corporate stock held by a West German bank.[3]

EMPLOYEES AND NEW OWNERS

With more corporations divesting business segments, employees and segment management find themselves with new supervisors, directions, corporate culture, standards of performance, and industrial expectations. The ideal divestiture would be a nonstrategic segment sale at full value to qualified buyers who would provide the employees with good opportunities to better their careers. Many corporations are taking an active interest in their broad responsibilities to communities, business relationships, and the future of the employees of the divested component. If the divested business is unsuccessful, the selling corporation's continuing operations and potential future divestitures will be negatively impacted because current employees will become concerned about their future instead of performing to the best of their ability.[4]

ANTITRUST ACTIVITY

Antitrust activity monitoring becomes very difficult when ownership frequently changes. Because the volume, size, and magnitude of both corporate acquisitions and divestitures has increased significantly in the last 20 years, governmental antitrust enforcement agencies have become overburdened with the changes. Periodic data comparisons become difficult to analyze. Because of sales, expense, and asset allocations within a corporation with several segments, market share, profit, and return on investment ratios and comparisons become indecisive without inside knowledge of the allocation relationships. When a complex corporation's financial statements are completely analyzed and the equally complex allocation methods unraveled, a divestiture requires the prior work to be modified and redone. Qualified enforcement staff is not available. Only the major, highly visible divestitures are reviewed for antitrust combinations. Enforcement analysis is concentrated on diversifications and acquisitions.

CORPORATE RAIDERS

Corporate raiders will become more important to the divestiture environment. Already T. Boone Pickens and Carl Icahn have gained a reputation as both corporate raiders and divestiture artists, although both have denied both descriptions. Divestiture announcements often have attracted the curiosity of these "raiders." When Firestone moved away from the low profit end of the tire business by closing low margin plants and selling others, it attracted the interest of Carl Icahn who began accumulating Firestone shares. Firestone chairman John Nevin commented, "We are more vulnerable to raiders for having reduced debt and raised cash, but we'll just have to live with it.

There is no way we can make this company more attractive to shareholders that won't at the same time make it more attractive to raiders."[5]

Another acquisition and then divestiture artist is Donald Kelly, chairman of Beatrice Co. Kelly has said he thinks food companies are top candidates to be his "targets." As he considered the purchase of Pillsbury Co., he was thought to be the best person to purchase Pillsbury and sell off its troubled restaurant business, including Burger King, for top dollar. "If anyone can wring premium prices out of not-so-premium businesses, it's Don Kelly," said a securities analyst.[6] His dream is to buy another large company and profitably break it up.

DIVESTITURE SUMMATION

What does the future hold for corporate divestitures? Corporate divestitures will be an alternative to be evaluated every time there is a change in corporate goals, performance or market. No longer is divestiture limited to bankruptcies and business failures.

Because of competition, business segments will be expected to meet internal standards of performance or face possible divestiture. Corporations are beginning to recognize the impact of major corporate changes on the locales where facilities are located. Concern for the morale of employees and management of the divested segment will become more important in divestiture decisions. With the rapid changes in corporate ownership of business components, governmental antitrust oversight will probably be inadequate. Complicating this situation is the re-emergence of corporate raiders. With all of the complications business faces in the future, change will become the norm, not the exception.

Notes

CHAPTER 1

1. J. Thackray, "The Perils of Restructuring," *Institutional Investor*, Sept. 1982, 98.
2. "Diversification Blues," *Mergers & Acquisitions*, May/June 1987, 14.
3. C. Scott, "Mergers Activity Fell 38% in 1987, W. T. Grimm Says," *Wall Street Journal*, 9 February 1988.
4. K. R. Andrews, *The Concept of Corporate Strategy* (Homewood, Ill.: Richard D. Irwin, 1980), 70.
5. R. Smith, "Merger Boom Defies Expectations," *Wall Street Journal*, 3 January 1989.

CHAPTER 2

1. K. Slater, "Avon to Sell Health Unit, Take A Charge," *Wall Street Journal*, 20 January 1988.
2. L. Landro, "Gulf & Western Plans to Sell Finance Firm, Build a Media Giant," *Wall Street Journal*, 10 April 1989.
3. L. Vignola, Jr., *Strategic Divestment* (New York: AMACON, 1974), 11.
4. "Schering-Plough Ends Accord to Buy Assets of Cooper Cos.," *Wall Street Journal*, 3 June 1988.
5. W. B. Tunstall, *Disconnecting Parties* (New York: McGraw-Hill, 1985), 15.

CHAPTER 3

1. Code IV, 59. Translation of A. H. March, reprinted in 23 *American Law Review* 261 (1889).

2. Moore 576, 72 English Rep. 769 (K. B. 1599).

3. 11 Co. Rep. 84b, 77 Eng. Rep. 1260 (K. B. 1602).

4. 1 P. Williams 181, 24 Eng. Rep. 347 (K. B. 1711).

5. C. Wilcox, "Competition and Monopoly in American Industry," *U.S. Temporary National Economic Committee Monograph No. 21* (1940), 68.

6. 51 Cong. Rec. 14217–21 (1914).

7. 51 Cong. Rec. 9173, 13665–66 (1914).

8. R. M. Calkins, *Anti-Trust: Guidelines for the Business Executive* (Homewood, Ill.: Dow Jones-Irwin, 1981), 27.

9. Cong. Rec., Vol. 95, p. 11, 486 (1949).

10. Cong. Rec., Vol. 96, p. 16, 452 (1950).

11. F. M. Scherer, *Industrial Market Structure and Economic Performance* (Boston: Houghton Mifflin, 1980), 124.

12. D. C. Bok, "Section 7 of the Clayton Act and the Merging of Law and Economics," *Harvard Law Review* 74 (1960), 226.

13. United States v. Philadelphia Bank, 374 U.S. 321 (1963).

14. United States v. Von's Grocery Co., 384 U.S. 272 (1966).

15. H. M. Applebaum, I. Scher, J. R. Loftis III, E. J. Bondurant II, eds., *Antitrust Law Developments* (Washington, D.C.: American Bar Assoc., 1975), 80.

CHAPTER 4

1. J. M. Clark, "Toward a Concept of Workable Competition," *American Economic Review*, June 1940, 241.

2. J. E. Meade, *The Theory of International Policy* (London: Oxford University Press, 1955), vol. 2, Trade and Welfare.

3. Scherer, *Industrial Market Structure*, 25.

4. K. G. Elzinga and W. Breit, *The Antitrust Penalties: A Study in Law and Economics* (New Haven: Yale University Press, 1976), 49.

5. M. Josephson, *The Robber Barons* (New York: Harcourt, 1962), 450.

6. United States v. E. I. du Pont de Nemours & Co., 366 U.S. 316, 326 (1961).

7. Testimony of Richard McLaren, S. Exec. Rep. No. 92–19, 92nd Cong., 2d Sess., pt. 4, 60 (1972).

8. United States v. International Salt Co., 332 U.S. 392, 401 (1947).

9. Elzinga and Breit, *The Antitrust Penalties*, 49.

10. O. E. Williamson, "Economics as an Antitrust Defense," *American Economic Review*, March 1968, 18–36.

11. United States v. Philadelphia Bank, 374 U.S. 321, 370 (1963).

12. Elzinga and Breit, *The Antitrust Penalties*, 102.

13. United States v. E. I. du Pont de Nemours & Co., 353 U.S. 586, 607–08 (1957).

14. 63 F.T.C. 1465, 1584 (1963).

15. United States v. E. I. du Pont de Nemours & Co., 366 U.S. 316 (1961).

16. United States v. Aluminum Co. of America, 247 F. Supp. 308 (E. D. Mo. 1964), aff'd per curiam, 382 U.S. 12 (1965).

17. 59 F.T.C. 614, 659 (1961).

18. W. J. Kolasky, Jr., P. A. Proger and R. T. Englert, Jr., "Anticompetitive Mergers: Prevention and Cure," in *Antitrust And Regulation*, F. M. Fisher, ed. (Cambridge: MIT Press, 1985), 51.

19. M. J. Green, B. C. Moored, Jr., and B. Wasserstein, *The Closed Enterprise System* (New York: Grossman, 1972), 346.

20. K. G. Elzinga, "The Antimerger Law: Pyrrhic Victories?" *Journal of Law & Economics*, December 1969, 43.

21. Ibid., 55–72.

22. M. Pfunder, D. Plaine, and A. M. Whittemore, "Compliance with Divestiture Orders under Section 7 of The Clayton Act: An Analysis of the Relief Obtained," *Antitrust Bulletin*, vol. 17, 1972, 19.

23. Kolasky, Proger and Englert, "Anticompetitive Measures," 55.

24. Calnetics Corp. v. Volkswagen of America, Inc., 348 F. Supp. 606 (C. D. Cal. 1972).

25. International Telephone & Telegraph Corp. v. General Telephone & Electronics Corp., 351 F. Supp. 1153 (D. Hawaii 1972).

26. K. M. Davidson, *Mega-Mergers: Corporate America's Billion-Dollar Takeovers* (Cambridge: Ballinger, 1985), p. 128.

CHAPTER 5

1. P. O. Steiner, *Mergers: Motives, Effects, Policies* (Ann Arbor: University of Michigan Press, 1975), 206–207.

2. Davidson, *Mega-Mergers*, 141.

3. L. Beman, "What We Learned from the Great Merger Frenzy," *Fortune*, April 1973, 70.

4. "Managers Who Are No Longer Entrepreneurs," *Business Week*, 30 June 1980, 78.

5. "The Pacrail Decision, New Ground Rules for Mergers," *Railway Age*, 29 November 1982, 10.

6. W. T. Grimm & Co., *Mergerstat Review*, 1982, 70–71.

7. "Republicans Reshape the FTC," *Business Week*, 5 June 1954, 43.

8. Green, Moore and Wasserstein, *The Closed Enterprise System*, 326.

9. Ibid., 31.

10. Ibid., 342.

11. A. H. Molod, "Forms and Paperwork," *The Mergers and Acquisitions Handbook*, M. L. Rock, ed., (New York: McGraw-Hill, 1987), 267.

CHAPTER 6

1. D. E. Rosenthal, S. E. Benson, and L. Chiles, "Doctrines and Problems Relating to U.S. Control of Transnational Corporate Concentration," *Corporate Concentration: National and International Regulation, Michigan Yearbook of International Legal Studies*, Vol. II (Ann Arbor: University of Michigan Press, 1981), 23.

2. *OECD Council Recommendation Document No. C(79)*, 1979, 154.

3. Testimony Concerning the Failing Company Defense Before the Subcommittee on Antitrust, Monopoly, and Business Rights of the Senate Committee on the Judiciary, 96th Cong., 1st Sess. (1979).

4. *Anglo-American Conflict of International Jurisdiction*, 13 Int. & Comp. L. Q. (1964), 1460.

5. European Economic Community Treaty, 298 U.N.T.S. No. 4300 (1958).

CHAPTER 7

1. R. Koenig, "Hercules Seeks New Labors to Perform," *Wall Street Journal*, 23 March 1989.

2. P. Norman, "Barclays Bank May Reduce U.S. Branches," *Wall Street Journal*, 7 January 1988.

3. "GE Completes Sale of Electronics Line to Thomson S. A.," *Wall Street Journal*, 4 January 1988.

4. "French Officials Outline Proposed Takeover Rules," *Wall Street Journal*, 8 March 1989.

5. *Extraterritoriality in Canada-United States Relations*, 63 Department State Bulletin, 425 (1970).

6. "W. R. Grace Plans $263 Million Sale of Fertilizer Firm," *Wall Street Journal*, 7 June 1988.

7. A. Sullivan, "Texaco Set to Sell West German Unit for $1.23 Billion," *Wall Street Journal*, 7 June 1988.

8. R. L. Rose, "Allegis to Sell Its Westin Unit for $1.35 Billion," *Wall Street Journal*, 28 October 1987.

9. "Sumitomo to Acquire Lumonics, a Maker of Lasers in Canada," *Wall Street Journal*, 28 March 1989.

10. R. L. Hudson, "Plessey Ruling Jolts British Defence Firms," *Wall Street Journal*, 24 April 1989.

11. J. Pereira, "Encore Agrees to Buy a Unit of Japan Firm," *Wall Street Journal*, 22 March 1989.

12. J. K. Brown, *Refocusing the Company's Business* (New York: The Conference Board, 1985), 15.

13. K. Ohmaw, "Only Triad Insiders Will Succeed," *The New York Times*, 2 September 1984.

14. Harvard Business School, *Case 4-385-065, Montedison S.p.A.* (Cambridge: Harvard University, 1984), 13.

15. C. Forman, "Chemical Bank to Sell London Mortgage Unit," *Wall Street Journal*, 24 March 1988.

16. J. S. Lublin, "Minorco Ends Hostile Bid to Acquire Consolidated Gold after U.S. Court Move," *Wall Street Journal*, 7 March 1989.

17. A. Pasztor and E. Lachica, "Pentagon is Handed Growing New Defense Role: Policing U.S. Corporate Takeovers from Abroad," *Wall Street Journal*, 8 March 1989.

18. L. Landro and D. Akst, "CBS Records' Sale to a Foreign Firm Is Grating on Some Industry Ears," *Wall Street Journal*, 20 November 1987.

19. J. S. Lublin, "With U.S. Takeovers Grown Expensive, Sir James Goldsmith Looks to Britain," *Wall Street Journal*, 7 March 1989.

20. M. R. Sesit and T. E. Ricks, "Mitsubishi Corp. Merger Activity in U.S. to Grow," *Wall Street Journal*, 2 March 1989.

21. T. Carrington, "Britain Blocks Elders Takeover of Big Brewer," *Wall Street Journal*, 22 March 1989.

CHAPTER 8

1. Brown, *Refocusing The Company's Business*, p. 33.

2. Ibid., p. 35.

3. Ibid., p. 2.

4. Ibid., p. 4.

5. "Philips to Reorganize World-Wide Business in Integrated Circuits," *Wall Street Journal*, 20 April 1989.

6. J. Levy and M. Sarnet, "Diversification, Portfolio Analysis and

the Uneasy Case for Conglomerate Mergers," *The Journal of Finance*, Sept. 1970, 801.

7. T. Petzinger, Jr., "Coastal May Sell Half of U.S. Oil Refining Assets," *Wall Street Journal*, 27 January 1988.

8. J. Thackray, "The Perils of Restructuring," *Institutional Investor*, Sept. 1982, 99.

9. L. Vignola, Jr., *Strategic Divestment* (New York: AMACON, 1974), 39.

10. K. R. Harrigan, "Exit Decisions in Mature Industries," *Academy of Management Journal*, Dec. 1982, 729.

11. Ibid.

12. B. R. Owen, "Factory Job Loss Passes 900: Region Hard Hit by Interco Plant Closings in Past Year," *Southeast Missourian*, Cape Girardeau, Mo., 29 March 1989.

13. I. M. Duhaime and J. H. Grant, "Factors Influencing Divestment Decision-Making: Evidence From A Field Study," *Strategic Management Journal*, Oct.-Dec. 1984, 318.

14. S. C. Gilmour, "The Divestment Decision Process," unpublished doctoral dissertation, Harvard Business School, 1973, 73.

15. J. F. Weston, "The Payoff in Mergers and Acquisitions," *The Mergers and Acquisitions Handbook*, M. L. Rock, ed. (New York: McGraw-Hill, 1987), 43.

16. Duhaime and Grant, "Factors Influencing Divestment," 313–314.

17. S. C. Diamond, ed., *Leveraged Buyouts* (Homewood, Ill.: Dow Jones-Irwin, 1985),7.

18. P. Yoshihashi, "Ramada Inc. Signs Agreement to Sell Its Callender Unit," *Wall Street Journal*, 27 March 1989.

19. Tunstall, *Disconnecting Parties*, p. 99.

CHAPTER 9

1. J. F. Weston, "The Payoff in Mergers and Acquisitions," *The Mergers and Acquisitions Handbook*, M. L. Rock, ed. (New York: McGraw-Hill, 1987), 31.

2. H. Harowitz and D. Halliday, "The New Alchemy: Divestment for Profit," *The Journal of Business Strategy*, Sept. 1984, 112.

3. L. J. Davis, "They Call Him Neutron," *Business Month*, March 1988, 27.

4. J. D. Steinbruner, *The Cybernetic Theory of Decision* (Princeton: Princeton University Press, 1974), 76.

5. I. M. Duhaime and C. R. Schwenk, "Conjectures On Cognitive

Simplification in Acquisition And Devestment Decision Making," *Academy of Management Review*, April 1985, 293.

6. Vignola, Jr., *Strategic Divestment*, 52.

7. L. C. Thurow, "The Productivity Problem," *Macro-Engineering in the Future*, F. P. Davidson and C. L. Meader, eds. (Boulder, Col.: Westview Press, 1982), 101.

8. D. J. Clarke and F. Gall, "Planned Divestment—A Five-Step Approach," *Long Range Planning*, Feb. 1987, 17.

9. Thackray, "The Perils of Restructuring," 99.

10. Ibid., 97.

11. "Change of Luck," *Forbes*, 8 April 1985, p. 14.

12. M. W. Brauchli and R. L. Hudson, "Ericsson Abandons Computer Division, Selling It to Nokia," *Wall Street Journal*, 21 January 1988.

13. K. Slater, "Avon To Sell Health Unit, Take a Charge," *Wall Street Journal*, 20 January 1988.

14. C. J. Clarke and F. Gall, "Planned Divestment—A Five-step Approach," *Long Range Planning*, Feb. 1987, 18.

15. M. S. Salter and W. A. Weinhold, *Diversification Through Acquisition* (New York: The Free Press, 1979), 22.

16. A. Michel and I. Shaked, "Does Business Diversification Affect Performance?" *Financial Management*, Winter 1984, 24.

17. T. Agins, "Campeau Will Sell $4.4 Billion in Assets to Pay for Costly Federated Acquisition," *Wall Street Journal*, 6 April 1988.

18. A. Corchado, "Primark Proposes to Spin Off Unit, Refocus Business," *Wall Street Journal*, 14 January 1988.

19. R. M. Kanter and T. K. Seggerman, "Managing Mergers, Acquisitions, and Divestitures," *Management Review*, Oct. 1986, 16.

20. R. N. Dubin, "Divestments," *FE*, 11 January 1986, 37.

21. B. Burrough, "Avery Inc. Says It Plans to Sell Chemical Firm," *Wall Street Journal*, 28 January 1988.

CHAPTER 10

1. C. Ferenback, "In Praise of the Leveraged Buyout," *Wall Street Journal*, 31 May 1984.

2. L. H. Clark, Jr., and A. L. Malabre, Jr., "Takeover Trend Helps Push Corporate Debt and Defaults Upward," *Wall Street Journal*, 15 March 1988.

3. A. Sullivan and J. Tanner, "Texaco May Sell Part of Refining Line in Europe," *Wall Street Journal*, 8 January 1988.

4. Clark and Malabre, "Takeover Trend."

5. A. Sullivan, "West German Firm Seeks Some Texaco Asset in Europe," *Wall Street Journal*, 18 March 1988.

6. J. D. Beazley and E. D. Lee, "USX To Sell Certain Assets to Lower Debt," *Wall Street Journal*, 21 June 1988.

7. C. Solomon and B. D. Solis, "Tenneco Puts Oil and Gas Unit on Block," *Wall Street Journal*, 26 May 1988.

8. D. Machalaba, "CSX Will Sell Oil, Gas Unit For $612 Million," *Wall Street Journal*, 23 March 1988.

9. T. Petzinger, Jr., "Coastal May Sell Half of U.S. Oil Refining Assets," *Wall Street Journal*, 27 January 1988.

10. "Carbide's Consumer Goods Sector to Be Sold," *C&EN*, 6 January 1986, 7.

11. R. Johnson, "Kelly And Kohlberg Kravis Are in Talks That Could Lead to Spinoff at Beatrice," *Wall Street Journal*, 2 February 1988.

12. J. Friedrick, "With Takeover Looming, Santa Fe Sells, Builds," *Investment Age*, 21 March 1988, 3.

13. F. Schwadel and R. Gibson, "General Mills Is Putting Up for Sale Talbots, Eddie Bauer Clothing Chains," *Wall Street Journal*, 8 January 1988.

14. J. Greenberg, "Getting Rid of a Good Thing," *Forbes*, 9 May 1983, 112.

15. "Chemical Bank to Sell London Mortgage Unit," *Wall Street Journal*, 24 March 1988.

16. "Second Thoughts On Diversity," *Mergers & Acquisitions*, Jan.-Feb., 1987, 12.

17. J. Friedrick, "With Takeover Looming, Santa Fe Sells, Builds," *Investment Age*, 21 March 1988, 22.

18. Thackray, "The Perils of Restructuring," 96.

19. F. Schwadel, "Ward's Sale Could Mean a Brother's Gain," *Wall Street Journal*, 29 January 1988.

20. F. Schwadel and R. Gibson, "General Mills Is Putting Up for Sale Talbots, Eddie Bauer Clothing Chains," *Wall Street Journal*, 8 January 1988.

21. R. G. Hamermesh, M. J. Anderson and J. E. Harris, "Strategies for Low Market Share Businesses," *Harvard Business Review*, Jan. 1979, 53.

22. "Layoffs, Restructuring: Olin, Pennwalt Unveil Massive Plan," *C&EN*, 7 October 1985, 4.

23. Vignola, *Strategic Divestment*, 6.

CHAPTER 11

1. M. R. Sesit and D. R. Sease, "Japanese Bring Strategic Determination to Foreign Grab for Rich U.S. Assets," *Wall Street Journal*, 21 March 1988.

2. C. W. Stevens, "Loral to Sell Two Divisions for $425 Million," *Wall Street Journal*, 28 March 1989.

3. K. R. Harrigan, "Exit Decisions in Mature Industries," *Academy of Management Journal*, Dec. 1982, 707.

4. R. B. Schmitt, "If An Investment Bank Says the Deal Is Fair, It May or May Not Be," *Wall Street Journal*, 10 March 1988.

CHAPTER 12

1. Thackray, "The Perils of Restructuring," 98.

2. A. B. Fisher, "The Decade's Worst Mergers," *Fortune*, 30 April 1984, 266.

3. Ibid., 270.

4. G. Slutsker, "Some Call It Restructuring," *Forbes*, 16 September 1985, 40.

5. C. Power, "Sell the Weak, Feed the Strong," *Forbes*, 18 November 1985, 235.

6. "Seeking The Right Blend," *Mergers & Acquisitions*, Nov.-Dec. 1986, 48.

7. M. S. Salter and W. A. Weinhold, *Diversification Through Acquisition* (New York: The Free Press, 1979), 45.

8. J. P. Miller, "Amfac Inc. to Sell Lamb-Weston Unit for $276 Million," *Wall Street Journal*, 4 April 1988.

9. C. Ansberry, "Sale of General Nutrition Inc. Is Considered," *Wall Street Journal*, 28 March 1989.

10. G. Hessol, "Debt Rating Revisions: Aftermath of Mergers," *Mergers & Acquisitions*, Winter 1985, 42.

11. B. Burrough, "Beatrice May Have to Be Sold in Pieces, Not in One Shot, Clouding Kelly's Plans," *Wall Street Journal*, 27 January 1988.

12. "Tyler Corp.: Discussions Are Held to Sell Its Reliance Universal Unit," *Wall Street Journal*, 10 April 1989.

13. L. H. Clark, Jr., and A. L. Malabre, Jr., "Takeover Trend Helps Push Corporate Debt and Defaults Upward," *Wall Street Journal*, 15 March 1988.

14. R. J. Clayton and W. Beranek, "Disassociations and Legal Combinations," *Financial Management*, Summer 1985, 25.

15. P. B. Brown, "Where Else Can You Go?" *Forbes*, 20 June 1983, 48.

CHAPTER 13

1. Tunstall, *Disconnecting Parties*, 144.
2. Ibid.
3. Dubin, "Divestments," 37.
4. Vignola, *Strategic Divestment*, 112.
5. R. M. Kanter and T. K. Seggerman, "Managing Mergers, Acquisitions, and Divestitures," *Management Review*, October 1986, 16.
6. D. Machalaba, "Sales of Short-Line Railroads Spread, Stall," *Wall Street Journal*, 3 June 1988.
7. "Layoffs, Restructuring: Olin, Pennwalt Unveil Massive Plan," *C&EN*, 7 October 1985, 4.
8. L. J. Davis, "They Call Him Neutron," *Business Month*, March 1988, 25–28.
9. Kanter and Seggerman, "Managing Mergers," 16.
10. D. Nees, "Increase Your Divestment Effectiveness," *Strategic Management Journal*, 30 April 1981, 120.
11. N. Barsky, "Sears Set To Sell Coldwell Banker to Malek Group," *Wall Street Journal*, 28 March 1989.
12. D. Solic, "Tenneco Is Creating Incentives to Keep Staff from Leaving Unit It Is Selling," *Wall Street Journal*, 8 June 1988.
13. R. J. Kudla and T. H. McInish, *Corporate Spin-Offs* (Westport, Conn.: Quorum Books, 1984), 22.
14. J. B. White, "Factory Towns Start to Fight Back Angrily When Firms Pull Out," *Wall Street Journal*, 8 March 1988.
15. Ibid.

CHAPTER 14

1. B. B. Gardner and D. G. Moore, *Human Relations in Industry* (Homewood, Ill.: Richard J. Irwin, 1964), 4th ed., 451.
2. T. A. Beehr, "Management of Work-Related Stress," *Current Issues in Personnel Management*, K. M. Rowland and G. R. Ferris, eds. (Boston: Allyn and Bacon, 1980), 307.
3. Ibid., 311.
4. S. Freud, "Draft L. Melancholia," *The Standard Edition of the Complete Psychological Works of Sigmund Freud*, S. Strachey ed., vol. 1 (London: Hogarth Press, 1966), 200.

5. G. F. Jacobson, *The Multiple Crises of Marital Separation And Divorce* (New York: Grune & Stratton, 1983), 15.

6. B. S. Dohrenwend and B. P. Dohrenwend, "Class and Race As Status-Related Sources of Stress," *Social Class*, S. Levine and N. Scotch, eds. (Chicago: Aldine, 1979).

7. M. Sherif and C. Sherif, *An Outline of Social Psychology* (New York: Harper & Row, 1956).

8. G. Allport, *The Nature of Prejudice* (Cambridge: Addison-Wesley, 1954).

9. J. Moritsugu and S. Sue, "Minority Status As a Stressor," *Preventive Psychology, Theory, Research And Practice*, R. D. Felner, L. A. Jason, J. N. Moritsugu, S. A. Farber, eds. (New York: Pergamon Press, 1983), 162.

10. S. Kobasa, "Personality and Resistance to Illness," *American Journal of Community Psychology*, July 1979, 413–423.

11. S. Parker and R. Kleiner, *Mental Illness in the Urban Negro Community* (New York: Free Press, 1966).

12. Moritsugu and Sue, "Minority Status," 168.

13. M. Seligman, *Helplessness: On Depression, Development and Death* (San Francisco: Freeman, 1975).

CHAPTER 15

1. R. S. Weiss, *Marital Separation* (New York: Basic Books, 1975).

2. E. M. Hetherington, M. Cox, and R. Cos, "The Aftermath of Divorce," *Mother-Child, Father-Child Interaction: Theory, Research and Prospect*, J. H. Stevens, Jr. and M. Matthews, eds. (New York: Academic Press, 1980).

3. S. Gettleman and J. Markowitz, *The Courage to Divorce* (New York: Simon and Schuster, 1974), 55.

4. Ibid., 66.

5. A. J. Cherlin, *Marriage, Divorce, Remarriage* (Cambridge: Harvard University Press, 1981), 89.

6. V. J. Derlega and L. H. Janda, *Personal Adjustment: The Psychology of Everyday Life* (Morristown, N.J.: Scott, Foresman, 1978), 105.

7. P. Selznick, "An Approach to A Theory of Bureaucracy," *American Sociological Review*, August 1943, 47.

8. J. D. Adams, "Guidelines for Stress Management and Life Style Changes," *The Personnel Administrator*, June 1979, 36.

9. B. J. Atkins, A. B. Meyer, and N. K. Smith, "Personal Care Attendants: Attitudes and Factors Contributing to Job Satisfaction," *Journal of Rehabilitation*, July/Aug./Sept. 1982, 24.

10. M. Lammert, "A Group Experience to Combat Burnout and Learn Group Process Skills," *Journal of Nursing Education*, June 1981, 43.

11. C. S. Laron, D. L. Gilbertson, and J. A. Power, "Therapist Burnout: Perspective on a Critical Issue," *Social Casework*, Nov. 1978, 564.

12. J. Adler and M. Gosnell, "Stress: How It Can Hurt," *Newsweek*, 21 April 1980, 106.

CHAPTER 16

1. J. J. Boddewyn, "Foreign and Domestic Divestment and Investment Decisions: Like or Unlike?" *Journal of International Business Studies*, Winter 1983, 29.

2. R. Cohen, "How to Divest," *Management Today*, May, 1983, 94.

3. C. J. Clarke and F. Gall, "Planned Divestment—A Five-Step Approach," *Long Range Planning*, Feb. 1987, 20.

CHAPTER 17

1. P. W. Barnes, "Tisch Favors CBS Records Unit Spinoff Rather Than Sale To Sony, Sources Say," *Wall Street Journal*, 10 November 1987.

2. Kudla and McInish, *Corporate Spin-Offs*, 24.

3. J. A. Miles and J. D. Rosenfeld, "The Effect of Voluntary Spin-Off Announcements on Shareholder Wealth," *The Journal of Finance*, 12 January 1983, 1597.

4. J. D. Rosenfeld, "Additional Evidence on the Relation Between Divestiture Announcements and Shareholder Wealth," *The Journal of Finance*, 12 January 1984, 1437.

5. L. Pittel, "The Parts and the Whole," *Forbes*, 25 March 1985, 264.

6. W. Cooper, "Playing The Spin-Off Game," *Institutional Investor*, June 1984, 150.

7. Ibid., 155.

8. "Ametek to Spin Off Some Units to Form a Separate Company," *Wall Street Journal*, 28 March 1988.

9. "Where's The Limit?" *Time*, 5 December 1988, 67.

10. Clark and Malabre, "Takeover Trend."

11. L. Caronia, "Seeking Financing: The Unsecured Leveraged Buyout," *Leveraged Buyouts*, S. C. Diamond, ed. (Homewood, Ill.: Dow Jones-Irwin, 1985), 62.

12. S. C. Diamond, ed., *Leveraged Buyouts* (Homewood, Ill.: Dow Jones-Irwin, 1985), 6.

13. Caronia, "Seeking Financing," 59.

14. H. J. Barry and R. A. Stratton, "Maximizing the Tax and Financial Benefits of Leveraged Buyouts," *Corporate Accounting*, Winter 1984, 16.

15. A. H. Chen and J. W. Kensinger, "Innovations in Corporate Financing: Tax-Deductible Equity," *Financial Management*, 31 December 1985, 47.

16. J. S. Schuchert, "The Art of the ESOP Leveraged Buyout," *Leveraged Buyouts* S. C. Diamond, ed. (Homewood, Ill.: Dow Jones-Irwin, 1985), 93.

17. "Soo Line Holds Talks to Consider Employee Buy-Out," *Wall Street Journal*, 28 January 1988.

18. "ESOP Borrowing Quadruples in '87," *Pensions & Investment Age*, 18 April 1988, 3.

19. J. Braden, "Royalty Trusts, a Closer at a New Concept," *Petroleum Independent*, 4 January 1984, 47–49.

CHAPTER 18

1. F. A. Lovejoy, *Divestment For Profit* (New York: Financial Executives Research Foundation, 1971), 9.

2. Thackray, "The Perils of Restructuring," 99.

3. "Grace to Buy Back Stock, Sell Retail Group," *Wall Street Journal*, 16 December 1985.

4. J. Long and M. H. Friedman, "The Seller's View of a Leveraged Buyout," *Leveraged Buyouts*, S. C. Diamond, ed. (Homewood, Ill.: Dow Jones-Irwin, 1985), 35.

5. Thackray, "The Perils of Restructuring," 98.

6. R. Johnson, "Kelly's Agreement on Sale of Juice Line Puts Him Closer to Acquisition Hunt," *Wall Street Journal*, 11 March 1988.

Bibliography

Adams, J. D. "Guidelines for Stress Management and Life Style Changes." *The Personnel Administrator* (June 1979).

Adler, J. and Gosnell, M. "Stress: How It Can Hurt." *Newsweek*, 21 April 1980.

Agins, T. "Campeau Will Sell $4.4 Billion in Assets to Pay for Costly Federated Acquisition." *Wall Street Journal*, 6 April 1988.

Allport, G. *The Nature of Prejudice.* Cambridge, Mass.: Addison-Wesley, 1954.

"Ametek To Spin Off Some Units To Form A Separate Company." *Wall Street Journal*, 28 March 1988.

Andrews, K. R. *The Concept of Corporate Strategy.* Homewood, Ill.: Richard D. Irwin, 1980.

Applebaum, H. M., Scher, I., Loftis III, J. R., Bondurant II, E. J., eds. *Antitrust Law Developments.* Washington, D.C.: American Bar Association, 1975.

Atkins, B. J., Meyer, A. B., and Smith, N. K. "Personal Care Attendants: Attitudes and Factors Contributing to Job Satisfaction." *Journal of Rehabilitation* (July/August/September 1982).

"Banks Know Too Much." *Business Month* (March 1988): 69.

Barnes, P. W. "Tisch Favors CBS Records Unit Spinoff Rather Than Sale to Sony, Sources Say." *Wall Street Journal*, 10 November 1987.

Barry, H. J., and Stratton, R. A. "Maximizing the Tax and Financial Benefits of Leveraged Buyouts." *Corporate Accounting* (Winter 1984): 16.

Barsky, N. "Sears Set to Sell Coldwell Banker to Malek Group." *Wall Street Journal*, 28 March 1989.

Beazley, J. D., and Lee, E. D. "USX to Sell Certain Assets to Lower Debt." *Wall Street Journal*, 21 June 1988.

Beehr, T. A. "Management of Work-Related Stress." *Current Issues in Personnel Management*, K. M. Rowland and G. R. Ferris, eds. Boston: Allyn and Bacon, 1980.

Beman, L. "What We Learned from the Great Merger Frenzy," *Fortune* (April 1973).

Boddewyn, J. J. "Foreign and Domestic Divestment and Investment Decisions: Like or Unlike?" *Journal of International Business Studies* (Winter 1983), 29.

Bok, D. C. "Section 7 of the Clayton Act and the Merging of Law and Economics." *Harvard Law Review*, 1960: 74.

Braden, J. "Royalty Trusts, A Closer Look at a New Concept." *Petroleum Independent*, 4 January, 1984, 47–49.

Brauchli, M. W., and R. L. Hudson. "Ericsson Abandons Computer Division, Selling It to Nokia." *Wall Street Journal*, 21 January 1988.

Brown, J. K. *Refocusing the Company's Business*. New York: Conference Board, 1985.

Brown, P. B. "Where Else Can You Go?" *Forbes*, 20 June 1983, 48.

Burrough, B. "Avery Inc. Says It Plans to Sell Chemical Firm." *Wall Street Journal*, 28 January 1988.

Burrough, B. "Beatrice May Have to Be Sold in Pieces, Not in One Shot, Clouding Kelly's Plans." *Wall Street Journal*, 27 January 1988.

Calkins, R. M. *Anti-Trust: Guidelines for the Business Executive*. Homewood, Ill.: Dow Jones-Irwin, 1981.

"Carbide's Consumer Goods Sector to Be Sold." *C&EN*, 6 January 1986, 7.

Caronia, L. "Seeking Financing: The Unsecured Leveraged Buyout." *Leveraged Buyouts*, S. C. Diamond, ed. Homewood, Ill.: Dow Jones-Irwin, 1985.

Carrinton, T. "Britain Blocks Elders Takeover of Big Brewer." *Wall Street Journal*, 22 March 1989.

"Change of Luck." *Forbes*, 8 April 1985, 14.

"Chemical Bank to Sell London Mortgage Unit." *Wall Street Journal*, 24 March 1988.

Chen, A. H., and Kensinger, J. W. "Innovations In Corporate Financing" Tax-Deductible Equity." *Financial Management*, 31 December 1985, 47.

Cherlin, A. J. *Marriage, Divorce, Remarriage*. Cambridge: Harvard University Press, 1981.

Clark, J. M. "Toward a Concept of Workable Competition," *American Economic Review* (June 1940).

Clark, L. H., Jr., and Malabre, A. L., Jr. "Takeover Trend Helps Push Corporate Debt and Defaults Upward." *Wall Street Journal*, 15 March 1988.

Clarke, C. J., and Gall, F. "Planned Divestment—A Five-Step Approach." *Long Range Planning*, (February 1987): 17.

Clayton, R. J., and Beranek, W. "Disassociations and Legal Combinations." *Financial Management* (Summer 1985): 25.

Cohen, R. "How to Divest." *Management Today* (May 1983), 94.

Cooper, W. "Playing the Spin-Off Game." *Institutional Investor* (June 1984): 155.

Corchado, A. "Primark Proposes to Spin Off Unit, Refocus Business." *Wall Street Journal*, 14 January 1988.

Davidson, K. M. *Mega-Mergers*. Cambridge: Ballinger, 1985.

Davis, L. J. "They Call Him Neutron." *Business Month* (March 1988): 27.

Derlega, V. J., and Janda, L. H. *Personal Adjustment: The Psychology of Everyday Life*. Morristown, N.J.: Scott, Foresman, 1978.

Diamond, S. C., ed. *Leveraged Buyouts*. Homewood, Ill.: Dow Jones-Irwin, 1985.

"Diversification Blues." *Mergers & Acquisitions*. (May-June 1987): 14.

Dohrenwend, B. S., and Dohrenwend, B. P. "Class and Race as Status-Related Sources of Stress." *Social Class*, S. Levine and N. Scotch, eds. Chicago: Aldine, 1979.

Dubin, R. N. "Divestments." *FE*, 11 January 1986, 37.

Duhaime, I. M., and Grant, J. H. "Factors Influencing Divestment Decision-Making: Evidence from a Field Study." *Strategic Management Journal* (October-December, 1984): 318.

Duhaime, I. M., and Schwenk, C. R. "Conjectures on Cognitive Simplification in Acquisition and Divestment Decision Making." *Adademy of Management Review* (April 1985): 293.

Elzinga, K. G. "The Antimerger Law: Pyrrhic Victories?" *Journal of Law & Economics* (December 1969).

Elzinga, K. G., and Breit, W. *The Antitrust Penalties: A Study in Law and Economics*. New Haven: Yale University Press, 1976.

"ESOP Borrowing Quadruples in '87." *Pensions & Investment Age*, 18 April 1988, 3.

Extraterritoriality in Canada–United States Relations. Department of State Bulletin 63, 1970.

Ferenback, C. "In Praise of the Leveraged Buyout." *Wall Street Journal*, 31 May 1984.

Fisher, A. B. "The Decade's Worst Mergers." *Fortune*, 30 April 1984, 266.

Forman, C. "Chemical Bank to Sell London Mortgage Unit." *Wall Street Journal*, 24 March 1988.

"French Officials Outline Proposed Takeover Rules." *Wall Street Journal*, 8 March 1989.

Freud, S. "Draft L. Melancholia." *The Standard Edition of the Complete Psychological Works of Sigmund Freud*, S. Strachey, ed. Vol. 1. London: Hogarth Press, 1966.

Friedrick, J. "With Takeover Looming, Santa Fe Sells, Builds." *Investment Age*, 21 March 1988, 3.

"GE Completes Sale of Electronics Line to Thomson S. A." *Wall Street Journal*, 4 January 1988.

Gilmour, S. C. "The Divestment Decision Process." Unpublished doctoral dissertation, Harvard Business School, 1973.

"Grace to Buy Back Stock, Sell Retail Group." *Wall Street Journal*, 16 December 1985.

Green, M. J., Moored, B. C., Jr., and Wasserstein, B. *The Closed Enterprise System*. New York: Grossman, 1972.

Greenberg, J. "Getting Rid of a Good Thing." *Forbes*, 9 May 1983, 112.

Grimm, W. T., Co. *Mergerstat Review*. Chicago: W. T. Grimm & Co., 1987.

Halloran, K. D. "The Impact of M&A Programs on Company Identity." *Mergers & Acquisitions* (Spring 1985): 62.

Hamermesh, R. G., Anderson, M. J., and Harris, J. E. "Strategies For Low Market Share Businesses." *Harvard Business Review* (January 1979): 53.

Harowitz, H., and Halliday, D. "The New Alchemy: Divestment for Profit." *The Journal of Business Strategy* (September 1984): 112.

Harrigan, K. R. "Exit Decisions in Mature Industries." *Academy of Management Journal* (December 1982): 707–729.

Hessol, G. "Debt Rating Revisions: Aftermath of Mergers." *Mergers & Acquisitions* (Winter 1985): 42.

Hetherington E. M., Cox, M., and Cos, R. "The Aftermath of Divorce." *Mother-Child, Father-Child Interaction: Theory, Research and Prospect*, J. H. Stevens, Jr. and M. Matthews, eds. New York: Academic Press, 1980.

Hudson, R. L. "Plessey Ruling Jolts British Defense Firms." *Wall Street Journal*, 24 April 1989.

Jacobson, G. F. *The Multiple Crises of Marital Separation And Divorce*. New York: Grune & Stratton, 1983.

Johnson, R. "Kelly and Kohlberg Kravis Are in Talks That Could Lead to Spinoff at Beatrice." *Wall Street Journal*, 2 February 1988.

Johnson, R. "Kelly's Agreement on Sale of Juice Line Puts Him Closer to Acquisition Hunt." *Wall Street Journal*, 11 March 1988.

Josephson, M. *The Robber Barons*. New York: Harcourt, 1962.

Kanter, R. M. and Seggerman T. K. "Managing Mergers, Acquisitions, and Divestitures." *Management Review* (October 1986): 16.

Kobasa, S. "Personality and Resistance to Illness." *American Journal of Community Psychology* (July 1979).

Koenig, R. "Hercules Seeks New Labors to Perform." *Wall Street Journal*, 23 March 1989.

Kolasky, W. J., Jr., Proger, P. A., and Englert, R. T. "Anticompetitive Mergers: Prevention and Cure," *Antitrust And Regulation*, Fisher, F. M. ed. Cambridge: MIT Press, 1985.

Kudla, R. J., and McInish, T. H. *Corporate Spin-Offs*. Westport, Conn.: Quorum Books, 1984.

Lammert, M. "A Group Experience to Combat Burnout and Learn Group Process Skills." *Journal of Nursing Education* (June 1981).

Landro, L. "Gulf & Western Plans to Sell Finance Firm, Build a Media Giant." *Wall Street Journal*, 10 April 1989.

Landro, L., and Akst, D. "CBS Records' Sale to a Foreign Firm Is Grating on Some Industry Ears." *Wall Street Journal*, 20 November 1987.

Laron, C. S., Gilbertson, D. L., and Power, J. A. "Therapist Burnout: Perspective on a Critical Issue." *Social Casework* (November 1978).

"Layoffs, Restructuring" Olin, Pennwalt Unveil Massive Plan." *C&EN*, 7 October 1985, 4.

Levy, J., and Sarnet, M. "Diversification, Portfolio Analysis and the Uneasy Case for Conglomerate Mergers." *The Journal of Finance* (September 1970): 801.

Long, J., and Friedman, M. H. "The Seller's View of a Leveraged Buyout." *Leveraged Buyouts*, S. C. Diamond, ed. Homewood, Ill.: Dow Jones-Irwin, 1985.

Lovejoy, F. A. *Divestment for Profit*. New York: Financial Executives Research Foundation, 1971.

Lublin, J. S. "Minorco Ends Hostile Bid to Acquire Consolidated Gold after U.S. Court Move." *Wall Street Journal*, 17 May 1989.

Lublin, J. S. "With U.S. Takeovers Grown Expensive, Sir James Goldsmith Looks To Britain." *Wall Street Journal*, 7 March 1989.

Machalaba, D. "CSX Will Sell Oil, Gas Unit for $612 Million." *Wall Street Journal*, 23 March 1988.

Machalaba, D. "Sales of Short-Line Railroads Spread, Stall." *Wall Street Journal*, 3 June 1988.

"Managers Who Are No Longer Entrepreneurs," *Business Week*, 30 June 1980.

Meade, J. E. *The Theory of International Policy*, Vol. 2, Trade and Welfare. London: Oxford University Press, 1955.

Michel, A., and Shaked, I. "Does Business Diversification Affect Performance?" *Financial Management* (Winter 1984): 24.

Miles, J. A., and Rosenfeld, J. D. "The Effect of Voluntary Spin-Off Announcements on Shareholder Wealth." *The Journal of Finance*, 12 January 1983, 1597.

Miller, J. P. "Amfac Inc., To Sell Lamb-Weston Unit for $276 Million." *Wall Street Journal*, 4 April 1988.

Molod, A. H. "Forms and Paperwork," *The Mergers and Acquisitions Handbook*. New York: McGraw-Hill, 1987.

Moritsugu, J., and Sue, S. "Minority Status as a Stressor." *Preventive Psychology, Theory, Research and Practice*, R. D. Felner, L. A. Jason, J. N. Moritsugu, and S. A. Farber, eds. New York: Pergamon Press, 1983.

Nees, D. "Increase Your Divestment Effectiveness." *Strategic Management Journal*, 30 April 1981, 120.

Norman, P. "Barclays Bank May Reduce U.S. Branches." *Wall Street Journal*, 7 January 1988.

Ohmae, K. "Only Triad Insiders Will Succeed." *The New York Times*, 2 September 1984.

Pasztor, A., and Lachica, E. "Pentagon Is Handed Growing New Defense Role: Policing U.S. Corporate Takeovers From Abroad." *Wall Street Journal*, 8 March 1989.

Parker, S., and Kleiner, R. *Mental Illness in the Urban Negro Community*. New York: Free Press, 1966.

Pereira, J. "Encore Agrees To Buy a Unit of Japan Firm." *Wall Street Journal*, 22 March 1989.

Perham, J. "Business Kicks Out the Turkeys." *Dun's Business Month* (September 1986): 30–34.

Petzinger, T., Jr. "Coastal May Sell Half of U.S. Oil Refining Assets." *Wall Street Journal*, 27 January 1988.

Pfunder, M., Plaine, D. and Whittemore, A. M. "Compliance with Divestiture Orders under Section 7 of the Clayton Act: An Analysis of the Relief Obtained," *Antitrust Bulletin*, vol. 17, 1972.

"Philips to Reorganize World-Wide Business in Integrated Circuits." *Wall Street Journal*, 20 April 1989.

Pittel, L. "Smaller Can Be Prettier." *Forbes*, 17 June 1985, 206–208.

Pittel, L. "The Parts and the Whole." *Forbes*, 25 March 1985, 264–268.

Power, C. "Sell the Weak, Feed the Strong." *Forbes*, 18 November 1985, 235.

Rahe, R. H. "Life Crisis and Health Change." *Psychotropic Drug Response: Advances In Prediction*, G. R. Wittenborn, ed. Springfield, Ill.: Charles B. Thomas, 1969.

Reis, J. P., and Cory, C. R. "The Fine Art of Valuation." *The Mergers and Acquisitions Handbook*, M. L. Rock, ed. New York: McGraw-Hill, 1987.

"Republicans Reshape the FTC," *Business Week*, 5 June 1954.

Rose, R. L. "Allegis to Sell Its Westin Unit for $1.35 Billion." *Wall Street Journal*, 28 October 1987.

Rosenfeld, J. D. "Additional Evidence on the Relation Between Divestiture Announcements and Shareholder Wealth." *The Journal of Finance*, 12 January 1984, 1437.

Rosenthal, D. E., Benson, S. E., and Chiles, L. "Doctrines and Problems Relating to U.S. Control of Transnational Corporate Concentration." *Corporate Concentration: National and International Regulation, Michigan Yearbook of International Legal Studies*, Vol. II. Ann Arbor: University of Michigan Press, 1981.

Salter, M. S., and Weinhold, W. A. *Diversification Through Acquisition*. New York: The Free Press, 1979.

Scherer, F. M. *Industrial Market Structure and Economic Performance*. Boston: Houghton Mifflin, 1980.

"Schering-Plough Ends Accord to Buy Assets of Cooper Cos." *Wall Street Journal*, 3 June 1988.

Schmitt, R. B. "If an Investment Bank Says the Deal Is Fair, It May or May Not Be." *Wall Street Journal*, 10 March 1988.

Schuchert, J. S. "The Art of the ESOP Leveraged Buyout." *Leveraged Buyouts*, S. C. Diamond, ed. Homewood, Ill.: Dow Jones-Irwin, 1985.

Schwadel, F. "Ward's Sale Could Mean a Brother's Gain." *Wall Street Journal*, 29 January 1988.

Schwadel, F., and Gibson, R. "General Mills Is Putting Up for Sale Talbots, Eddie Bauer Clothing Chains." *Wall Street Journal*, 8 January 1988.

Scott, C. "Mergers Activity Fell 38% in 1987, W. T. Grimm Says." *Wall Street Journal*, 9 February 1988.

"Second Thoughts on Diversity." *Mergers & Acquisitions,* (January-February 1987): 12.

"Seeking The Right Blend." *Mergers & Acquisitions,* (November-December, 1986): 48.

Seligman, M. *Helplessness: On Depression, Development and Death,* San Francisco: Freeman, 1975.

Sesit, M. R., and Ricks, T. E. "Mitsubishi Corp. Merger Activity in U.S. to Grow." *Wall Street Journal,* 2 March 1989.

Sesit, M. R., and Sease, D. R. "Japanese Bring Strategic Determination to Foreign Grab for Rich U.S. Assets." *Wall Street Journal,* 21 March 1988.

Sherif, M. and Sherif, C. *An Outline of Social Psychology.* New York: Harper & Row, 1956.

Slater, K. "Avon to Sell Health Unit, Take a Charge." *Wall Street Journal,* 20 January 1988.

Slutsker, G. "Some Call It Restructuring." *Forbes,* 16 September 1985, 40.

Smith, R. "Merger Boom Defies Expectations." *Wall Street Journal,* 3 January 1989.

Solic, D. "Tenneco Is Creating Incentives to Keep Staff from Leaving Unit It Is Selling." *Wall Street Journal,* 8 June 1988.

Solomon, C., and Solis, B. D. "Tenneco Puts Oil and Gas Unit on Block." *Wall Street Journal,* 26 May 1988.

"Soo Line Holds Talks to Consider Employee Buy-Out." *Wall Street Journal,* 28 January 1988.

Steinbruner, J. D. *The Cybernetic Theory of Decision.* Princeton, N.J.: Princeton University Press, 1974.

Steiner, P. O. *Mergers: Motives, Effects, Policies.* Ann Arbor: University of Michigan Press, 1975.

Stevens, C. W. "Loral to Sell Two Divisions for $425 Million." *Wall Street Journal,* 28 March 1989.

Sullivan, A. "Texaco Set to Sell West German Unit for $1.23 Billion." *Wall Street Journal,* 7 June 1988.

Sullivan, A. "West German Firm Seeks Some Texaco Asset in Europe." *Wall Street Journal,* 18 March 1988.

Sullivan, A., and Tanner, J. "Texaco May Sell Part Of Refining Line In Europe." *Wall Street Journal,* 8 January 1988.

Thackray, J. "The Perils of Restructuring." *Institutional Investor* (September 1982): 98–99.

"The Pacrail Decision, New Ground Rules for Mergers," *Railway Age,* 29 November 1982.

Thurow, L. C. "The Productivity Problem." *Macro-Engineering In The*

Future, F. P. Davidson and C. L. Meader, eds. Boulder: Westview Press, 1982.

Tunstall, W. B. *Disconnecting Parties*. New York: McGraw-Hill, 1985.

Vignola, L., Jr. *Strategic Divestment*. New York: AMACON, 1974.

Weiss, R. S. *Marital Separation*. New York: Basic Books, 1975.

Weston, J. F. "The Payoff in Mergers and Acquisitions," *The Mergers and Acquisitions Handbook*, M. L. Rock, ed. New York: McGraw-Hill, 1987.

"Where's The Limit?" *Time*, 5 December 1988, 67.

White, J. B. "Factory Towns Start to Fight Back Angrily When Firms Pull Out." *Wall Street Journal*, 8 March 1988.

Wilcox, C. "Competition and Monopoly in American Industry." *U.S. Temporary National Economic Committee Monograph No. 21*, 1940.

Williamson, O. E. "Economies as an Antitrust Defense," *American Economic Review* (March 1968).

"W. R. Grace Plans $263 Million Sale of Fertilizer Firm." *Wall Street Journal*, 7 June 1988.

Index

About the Author

RICHARD J. SCHMIDT is Dean of the College of Business Administration at Southeast Missouri State University.